*Four Portraits
and One Subject:*

Bernard DeVoto

Four Portraits
and One Subject:

Bernard DeVoto

The Historian

BY CATHERINE DRINKER BOWEN

The Writer

BY EDITH R. MIRRIELEES

The Citizen

BY ARTHUR M. SCHLESINGER, JR.

The Personality

BY WALLACE STEGNER

WITH

A BIBLIOGRAPHY OF HIS WRITINGS

PREPARED BY JULIUS P. BARCLAY

WITH THE COLLABORATION

OF ELAINE HELMER PARNIE

PS
3507
D39
Z6

1 9 6 3

HOUGHTON MIFFLIN COMPANY BOSTON

The Riverside Press Cambridge

Contents

Introduction by Wallace Stegner

THIS BOOK is the extended consequence of a feeling that many people had after Bernard DeVoto's death — the feeling that a man of such vitality, intelligence, and variety simply does not die when he dies. DeVoto during his life was present in a lot of the salons and most of the street fights of the intellectual life of America, and he left behind him not merely a shelf of continuingly influential books, but many strongly influenced minds. And none of us whose thinking he profoundly affected can think of him as ended.

That sense of his persistent importance is not confined to his personal friends. Casual readers felt it and still feel it. It took no more than a suggestion to bring his library and papers to Stanford. Thanks to the generosity of Mr. Edward Heller and the promptness of university officials, I was telephoning Avis DeVoto with an offer within two hours of the time I had the idea. And Mrs. DeVoto, in accepting the offer, phrased for us the reason for our enthusiastic unanimity. She had been dreading, she said, to see Benny's mind dispersed.

He has not been dispersed. At least his mind's work-shop is intact, somewhat tidier and more publicly available than when he was using it, and supplemented by corre-spondence and other memorabilia contributed by dozens of correspondents and friends. In these books and papers it is possible to examine not only his finished ideas but the processes of their evolution and the raw materials out of which they were made. Because DeVoto was historian, novelist, pamphleteer, teacher, essayist, short story writer, and critic — he called himself a literary department store — the processes of his mind are nearly as instructive as its products.

When, after several years of assembling and ordering, the DeVoto Papers were opened to general scholarly use, Julius Barclay, the Director of Special Collections at Stan-ford and the compiler of the bibliography in this volume, felt that there should be an occasion. Again, the sugges-tion was enough. Four of DeVoto's friends, Catherine Drinker Bowen, Edith Mirrielees, Arthur Schlesinger, Jr., and myself, discussed him as he had seemed to us; and if, in this composite portrait, we have made him in the like-ness of a rope, a spear, a tree, or a wall, that is what he gets for being so complex a thing as an elephant.

I speak only for myself, but I do not think that any of us would pretend we have captured Benny here between covers. If we have expressed fragments of his diversity we shall have done all we intended or hoped. The his-tories, the essays, the often angry and frequently noble pamphleteering articles, express him as he would most want to be expressed. Hence the bibliography. But it seems proper that the bibliography should be surrounded, as Benny himself liked to be, by a small circle of friends.

The Historian

by
Catherine Drinker Bowen

BERNARD DEVOTO was my valued friend. I am among the host of writers who came to him for advice, for criticism, and for general renewal of spirit. In letters and by word of mouth DeVoto and I shouted at each other. But always, in the end, I sat still and listened to what he had to say. And after each encounter, I came away rejoicing in the existence of that vivid, generous, and diabolically intelligent presence.

Mr. DeVoto had much influence on me as a writer. He still has. Very often, when I have composed a page on which I look with favor, I hear a voice within. "What," it asks, "would DeVoto think of that?" He is looking over my shoulder, his big spectacles level with my eye. I go back, rewrite the passage — an exercise known to DeVoto as "just running it through your typewriter again." Out come the adjectives, the passive verb turns active, the sentences tighten and compress. As we grow older, DeVoto told me, our style becomes simpler, or it should. Age, he said, reduces us to the ultimate simplicities. There is not time left for frill and ornament. When he died he was only fifty-eight, and when he spoke to me of age he could not have been more than fifty-five.

What a handsome shelf of histories DeVoto has given us! *Mark Twain's America* — which surely must be counted as history; *The Year of Decision; Across the Wide Missouri; The Course of Empire.* And finally, his superb edition of *The Journals of Lewis and Clark.* Critics have grouped the three central books as a trilogy; DeVoto himself referred to them that way. For my part I cannot separate them from the others. I see the five books as composing the wide arc and panorama of DeVoto's thesis: the westward movement of a people, the settling and seeding of a continent, the culture that flowered therefrom, and the slow, episodic acceptance of the federal idea. From the Atlantic to the Pacific, a federal union — impossible, romantic, necessitous conception which today we know as the United States of America. Nobody thought we could do it; in Europe it had not been achieved on anything approaching such a scale. Even Thomas Jefferson supposed that, following the Louisiana Purchase, we might be needing two republics, one east of the Rocky Mountains and one west. "As a historian," wrote DeVoto, "I have interested myself in the growth among the American people of the feeling that they were properly a single nation between two oceans; in the development of what I have called the continental mind."

Bernard DeVoto was haunted by that idea and by his vision of how it came to pass, geographically, culturally, agriculturally, anthropologically. The continental reality, he called it. He thought and wrote of this reality in terms of history, biography, fiction, poetry (written when he was very young). He even composed a play about the Mormons. And there is, it may be said, another word for the condition of a haunted man. Some people call it inspiration.

As for DeVoto's "place among American historians," let me say at once that he is not to be placed, classified, or categorized. There is no historian like him and no histories like his. His thinking was direct, ruthless, wholly his own, and because of it, less original men feared him. He was a fighter for public causes, for conservation of our natural resources, for freedom of the press and freedom of thought. The world knew him better in that guise, perhaps, than as a historian. Yet I shall make it my business to speak of DeVoto the fighter. For this trait — call it pugnacity, call it passion, hot blood, or a high-beating heart — this trait it is which informs and animates DeVoto's historical writing, from his early essays on the Mormons to his last words about the great captains, Lewis and Clark.

When DeVoto said the word "west," he did not mean, of course, the states to which John Randolph of Roanoke referred when he spoke of "those geographical *expressions* beyond the Alleghenies." DeVoto meant the desert west, the arid, thin-soiled Rocky Mountain west which begins, he said, "at that place where the average annual rainfall drops below twenty inches." All of DeVoto's books, including his first three novels, are concerned with the movement west. *Mark Twain's America*, the first of his books of history, announced his lifelong theme. It opens in 1835 with "The New Jerusalem," as DeVoto called it — that western Zion envisioned by men of piety and men whose god was gold. Mark Twain's parents left their eastern home to settle there. "The migration," wrote DeVoto, "was under way. Its great days were just around the turn of spring — and an April restlessness, a stirring in the blood, a wind from beyond the oak's openings, spoke of the prairies, the great desert, and the western sea. The common man fled westward. A thirsty land swallowed him insatiably. There is no comprehending the frenzy of the American folk-migration. God's gadfly had stung us mad."

After *Mark Twain's America*, eleven crowded years went by before DeVoto wrote his second volume of social history. *The Year of Decision* is perhaps the most absorbing of DeVoto's books, with its account of the Donner party's fearful march across the desert and Rocky Mountains, a story of starvation, courage, bestiality, faith, and almost incredible endurance. *Across the Wide Missouri* came next. Magnificently illustrated with colored reproductions of contemporary paintings by Alfred Jacob Miller, it won both the Pulitzer and the Bancroft prizes. *Across the Wide Missouri* sets out to tell of the early fur trade — "how it helped to shape our heritage," writes DeVoto, "what its relation was to the western expansion of the United States, most of all how the mountain men lived."

This "most of all" is what brings the book alive. And it is an extraordinary reconstruction. Mountain men, free trappers, the long hunter and the hapless tenderfoot — we see them, hear them talk, share their camp, their appalling meals of buffalo guts raw or roasted, their dangers and their hero-sized sprees when the trail ends in safety. We learn more about Indians than we thought we cared to know. Warriors and their squaws confront us, not as Uncas or Hiawatha or Minnehaha, Laughing Water, but as they were actually seen, heard, and smelled by travelers in the wagon trains. Trappers traded furs with the tribes, killed them skulking at night beyond the campfire, or bought the favors of the young squaws. DeVoto hated romanticism about Indians, "the squash blossom in the hair and talk about the plumed serpent." It did not help, he said, "to be precious about the rain dance and the mystical awareness that neolithic savages are supposed to have." He hated also the overintellectual approach and declared that anyone who thinks of Indians as the Amerinds is not going to add much to our literature.

These are gorgeous books, all three. No less a word will do. They are rich, strong, filled with color and movement. Also they are long books, jammed with fact. Not infrequently there is repetition, a page or two or three which the reader is inclined to skip. This is a fault of all long books; I am not even sure that it is a fault. DeVoto, going over a lengthy book manuscript of mine, told me not to worry about including a dull page now and then, of connective matter or exposition or suchlike. "Give the reader time to breathe," he said. Actually, DeVoto's method achieved an even more subtle purpose. His books of history have — as Alfred Knopf once pointed out — an interwoven architecture, a deliberate movement from theme to theme. The narrative could have proceeded in a straight line, direct from start to finish. But DeVoto chose the more difficult and far more effectual method of taking several stories or themes and carrying them along, parallel. This does not make for careless reading. He who wishes to travel with DeVoto will have to keep his head; the journey will not be easy. In one of his prefaces, DeVoto confesses the purpose of his books: "to tell the story in such a way that the reader may realize the far western experience — which is part of our cultural experience — as personal experience."

Let readers say if he succeeded. I know one reader who has had to put these books aside at times, when the terror and the suffering needed surcease. There is small doubt about this being a shared experience. From Massachusetts, from Virginia, we travel with these humble men and women as they launch their wagon trains over the Alleghenies, through the forests and grasslands to where the trails run west from Council Bluffs or Independence — across the Blue, across the Nishnabotna, across the wide Missouri.

Throughout the books I have discussed, DeVoto's history has been frankly episodic, sectional, a string of vivid anecdotes comprising in space a continent and in time a generation or two. But in his next and fourth volume, *The Course of Empire*, DeVoto swings far backward in chronology and ties the long threads together. Boldly his narrative opens in the eighth century with that missionary archbishop who set out over the Atlantic — the Sea of Darkness — and founded, on the legendary island of Antilia, the seven radiant cities of God. The narrative ends in the year 1805, with a line from the notebook of Captain Clark, Meriwether Lewis' partner. On a rainy November morning, Captain Clark looks westward from his mountain camp and writes, in his own phonetic spelling, "Ocian in view. O! the joy."

After this book, DeVoto was bound to edit *The Journals of Lewis and Clark*. And by now, he knew these journal writers and these journeys as he knew the back of his hand or the Wasatch Mountains and Weber Canyon, where he roamed as a boy. In the summer of 1946 he had even followed, in person, the actual trails taken by Lewis and Clark. His edition of the journals is authoritative and final. And it is the best kind of historical reading, notes and all. An introduction, vigorous, thick-packed, explains Jefferson's purpose in dispatching the expedition and the political and social urgencies involved. Published in 1955, the book's final chapter is called "The Home Stretch." One could wish the title had not proved, for DeVoto himself, so tragically symbolic.

How did DeVoto come to write these books? What conditions of birth, background, and experience shaped his style and caused him to be a man thus haunted? In truth one felt behind this man a compulsion so strong that, but for an essential health and integrity — and a wife like

Helen Avis MacVicar DeVoto — his talent might have torn him wide apart.

DeVoto's father, Florian Bernard DeVoto, of Ogden, Utah, was the son of an Italian cavalry officer; his mother was the daughter of a Mormon pioneer. (DeVoto liked to say that he was born of an apostate Mormon and an apostate Roman Catholic.) At high school he had a job as a reporter for the Ogden *Evening Standard*. When he was sixteen the paper published his first printed piece, which bore no less a title than "The Reasonableness of World-Wide Conciliation." DeVoto entered the University of Utah, but when four members of the faculty were dismissed for unorthodox opinions, the young sophomore left and finished his education at Harvard. He came west again to teach in Wisconsin, but in his late twenties picked up and migrated eastward to Cambridge, Massachusetts, where he spent the rest of his life, except for two years in New York as editor of the *Saturday Review of Literature*. To my best knowledge and belief he never went farther from the borders of the U.S.A. than a few miles into Canada.

For me, the significant facts of this brief biography are, first, that DeVoto was born and raised in Utah; and, second, that he was a novelist before he was a historian. DeVoto was conscious of his debt to this literary apprenticeship. The fore matter to *The Year of Decision* carries a page and a half of thanks to those men and women who helped with its preparation — scholars, librarians, critical readers of manuscript. "Finally," says DeVoto, "I acknowledge that I could not possibly have written the book if I had not had periodic assistance from Mr. John August."

John August was the pen name signed by DeVoto to four novels, all of them serialized in *Collier's* magazine. Perhaps DeVoto meant financial assistance. John August, he used to say, paid the rent. But I prefer to read further into that wry little statement. Four novels signed by John August, five signed by DeVoto. I have read them all, from *The Crooked Mile* (1924) to *Mountain Time* (1947). I do not care for them, except as their writing taught DeVoto to write history, gave him facility, cut the bonds imposed by the academic training and tradition, and allowed him to move freely and exuberantly within the prescribed circle of historic fact. DeVoto is not the first historian or the last to come to his craft by way of fiction writing.

I do not know whether, at the outset, DeVoto thought of himself primarily as a novelist. I suspect that he did. In the Widener Library I read a critical review written in 1928 by a college professor who took DeVoto very seriously as a novelist. DeVoto was early aware of his confessed literary aim — to make America realize the western pioneer experience. Very likely he thought, at the outset, that it could best be done by fiction. He wrote novels periodically from 1924 to 1947, meanwhile casting about for other ways to express his theme. When he was engaged in a novel, DeVoto never talked to me about it; our conversations concerned historical writing. Therefore I am only guessing when I say that I think he suffered during the composition of these novels. When he fell short of aim DeVoto knew it; he did not spare self-criticism. In 1934, I was trying to buy his early novels and he wrote me, "Be warned, my juvenilia are ungodly lousy, and *The Crooked Mile* is the most terrible and amusing of them all." Twenty years later, DeVoto told a friend that he had solved his life once he gave up fiction writing.

Yet it was his novels, I believe, which taught DeVoto how to lead his readers through the wilderness of historical fact. The writing of fiction is a relentless discipline, and in its exercise an author learns techniques which can serve the historian well. He learns, for instance, to manipulate scene and time, learns how to move his characters about, get them from the back porch into the kitchen. He learns how to arrange his material into a pattern or "plot," so that the reader can follow. History also has its patterns, implicit in the material and only awaiting the artist's eye to perceive and bring them out. In the management of historical time, DeVoto was especially skillful. Let me recommend to you page 64 of *The Course of Empire*, where DeVoto ranges freely across four hundred years, philosophically as well as chronologically — a difficult thing to do without throwing the reader into hopeless confusion. The chapter is entitled "The Spectrum of Knowledge," the year is 1540:

> The Spaniards set out to conquer Cibola, a country whose cities were walled with gold, on the word of one man that five emeralds which were not emeralds had come from there.

They set out to conquer the even richer Quivira on the word of one man that the common supper plates were made of gold . . . Mankind has always thought objectively about the exchange of goods and the skills of warfare, but not much else. Francis Bacon's *Advancement of Learning* was published in 1605. Not many men in that year, or in 1540, cared or were able to inquire into the nature of evidence, or to advance learning by perceiving that there is a difference between the real and the unreal. Not many care or can now, but there were fewer in an age when the medieval mind, with its daily bread of miracle and sorcery, had only begun to turn away from wonder. My son's wife's brother knows a man who slew a unicorn and in the country of Prester John are men with three legs. Men whose heads do grow beneath their shoulders, men with the heads of dogs, and trees whose fruit is living sheep.

The paragraph is itself material for a chapter, almost for a book. We have ranged from 1540 to 1605, back to the medieval mind and forward to the twentieth century. Not many care *now*, DeVoto wrote, thus letting us guess which side he was on — the Baconian side of fact, induction, and experience.

Or let us observe a still different manipulation and effect, from *Mark Twain's America*. The narrative begins and ends with Halley's comet. For DeVoto it was sheer luck that Samuel Clemens was born with the comet in 1835 and died with its return in 1910. But it was the kind of luck which comes only to the initiated, to an artist who is so absorbed in his subject that everything feeds it. Everything such a man sees, reads, hears is referred to that subject — rejected if immaterial, and if pertinent, retained with almost insane tenacity until the moment for its proper use.

Beginning and ending *Mark Twain's America* with the comet had nothing to do with historiography or scholarship. It had to do with the art of writing; it was a writer's device. Good art, the best art, is full of such devices — circus turns and sleights of hand which invariably succeed. They come off: five rabbits emerge from the hat when we looked for only one; the colored balls fly through the air and land, each in its cup. It requires technique as well as talent to break the barriers between ourselves and the past. By the time I met him in 1934, Benny DeVoto was an old pro and proud of it. By no means a professional historian, but a professional writer who referred to himself in print as "a historian, riding on the commuter's local." Not, DeVoto implied, a dweller in the sacred city, in the pure temple of the guild historian. And indeed DeVoto wandered far beyond the historian's conventional territory. For twenty years he supplied *Harper's Magazine* with monthly pieces for their department called "The Easy Chair." The Stanford Library has a list of his published articles and editorials that covers fifty-one sheets of typewriter-sized paper. DeVoto taught at Harvard, and it was not history he taught, but writing; he taught also at the Bread Loaf Writers' Conference in Vermont. "I am," he told his wife once, "a literary department store."

He had learned how to write by writing and his experience in the field was wider than most men's. Novelists are commonly more skillful than historians in describing individuals. It is a novelist's nature to be interested in people. And his descriptions have to start from scratch. His characters are created out of air, with no contemporary portraits to help, such as the historian has — no descriptions in diaries or family correspondence. The novelist simply sits down and sweats it out until his man comes alive on the page.

DeVoto knew this. When he had a historical character to describe he assembled the documents, absorbed them thoroughly, and then started again from the beginning, *ab ovo,* as it were. Read his description of "that gnarled grizzly-hunter, Joe Meek." Or of Jim Bridger, mountain man, called Old Gabe, whose habit it was to wake in the night, throw buffalo ribs on the fire, eat hearty, and "sing Injun to himself with a tin pan accompaniment." (Captain Humfreville read *Hiawatha* aloud by the campfire and Old Gabe hated it; he never seen no Indians like them, he said.) Read DeVoto's description of the Reverend Samuel Parker, gentle scholar bound west by pack train from Middlefield, Massachusetts. Or his paragraph about the two first white women ever to cross America. Eliza Spaulding, "in heavy boots and swathed by yards of skirt," riding sidesaddle on the South Pass when trappers and Indians galloped whooping down to greet the caravan. "Eliza," writes DeVoto, "tall, naturally thin and emaciated by travel and illness, dark-haired, sallow under tan, frightened and appalled by the uproar of hospitality. And Narcissa Whitman who was neither frightened nor appalled — she was delighted. A smaller woman than Eliza but by no means emaciated, the period's ideal in womanly curves, blue-eyed, tanned now but memorably blond. Men always remembered her face and red-gold hair. Men in fact remembered Narcissa, and though she was dedicated to God's service she was charged with a magnetism whose nature no one could mistake."

For a historian, this is emancipated language. DeVoto is riding the commuter's local. We see these young women, we know them after a few sentences. DeVoto could do it more subtly when he chose, and when the occasion called for subtlety. Hear him on the flaming orator of the 1890's, William Jennings Bryan. Many historians had already described Bryan, who therefore could be disposed of with one hand. "Six years earlier," writes DeVoto (it does not matter in what connection); "Six years earlier the sonorous, fraudulent voice of an eater of wild honey in the hills had quieted a Chicago convention hall . . . 'You shall not crucify mankind upon a cross of gold.' "

That is all, and it is enough. It assumes a certain amount of historical knowledge on the reader's part. But even without such knowledge, one catches DeVoto's meaning. "An eater of wild honey in the hills." DeVoto's early training in the Bible served him well. Years ago, I wrote him, "Those black-haired people who brought you up have read Scripture to you, Benny. What else would put such a roll, such a punch into your sentences?"

It is when DeVoto writes of the Mormons that his Biblical phraseology serves him best. Joseph Smith he called a man "drunk on God and glory"; Brigham Young, "an organizer of the kingdom on this earth . . . the one Mormon of history who knew how to laugh." When finally the Mormons triumphed over hardship and over continued hostility, and their city was secure and their credit good, "The Saints," wrote DeVoto, "had come into the inheritance promised them, their rivals had fallen away, their enemies had been trodden under foot or converted into business partners, their wars were ended forever, Israel was secure, the stake of Zion had been driven fast."

The DeVoto vocabulary was wide and he liked to use it; the tools of his trade felt good to his hand. The word "parallax" was a favorite, the word "eidolon" and terms like "mitosis," from the biologist's lexicon. Mark Twain he spoke of as "a maculate and episodic genius," and a certain phrase which DeVoto disliked carried, he said, "a slight taxonomic emphasis on the adjective." Yet DeVoto was never carried away by his own virtuosity. He did not succumb to the temptation to be abstruse, to skip three arguments and confuse his readers with the clever man's ellipses. DeVoto wrote history in a conversational style, always colorful, often polemical, very difficult to achieve, and wonderfully adapted to what he had to say. There was no room for pompousness. DeVoto addressed his readers as if they were his equals — even when he was blasting off at the enemy, which was not infrequent. When occasionally he did slip into one of those large, neophilosophical statements that make for pomposity, DeVoto recognized his error and pulled up short. "The genius of the American people . . ." Thus, in "The Easy

Chair," he began a paragraph — and quickly corrected himself. "No," he wrote, "start that one over. The vigor of our democratic system and the size and richness of our continental empire . . ."

The writing of history needs humor, and humility. And it needs affection, a fellow feeling for mankind, a perception of motivation in human beings. It needs, in short, the novelist's eternal preoccupation with the whys and wherefores of men's actions. DeVoto had this preoccupation. Catch him any time when he was not working and he was ready to talk for hours about why a woman had said a certain thing to her child, or why a young man had not defended himself against attack. His books speak often and lovingly of "the damned human race" — a phrase he got from Mark Twain. And it was a phrase neither comic nor ironic. Man's fate is hopeless, he is doomed, and he endures his fate with valor. This is DeVoto's belief, the point of his departure and of his return. And it is the point where his fever rises when he sees this belief questioned, as with Sinclair Lewis, "who spent his talents," said DeVoto, "in writing fiction that was conceived to show the contemptibility of American life." *Mark Twain's America* is a fighting book, a book with a thesis. DeVoto has an ax to grind and he grinds it till the wheel screams. His pugnacity has been deplored by his admirers as well as by his detractors. He himself admitted in print that one day he might rewrite *Mark Twain's America* and leave out the blasts against Mr. Van Wyck Brooks. I am glad he never did, because I believe that without anger, this book would have fallen short of greatness. Anger drives these pages forward. Anger brings the book to life.

What was Bernard DeVoto mad at? His critics protested that they did not know, they could not find out. DeVoto, they implied, was just plain born angry, and arrogant, and insulting. What, they demanded, was his thesis? What was he defending and why did it need defense? "Has he a secret?" Edmund Wilson asked, in the *New Republic*. "If so, let him stand and unfold himself. What does he want?"

DeVoto made plain enough what he wanted. I fail to see why Edmund Wilson didn't recognize it, and Sinclair Lewis, when he wrote, in the *Saturday Review of Literature*, the diatribe entitled "Fools, Liars and Mr. DeVoto." Bernard Augustine DeVoto of Ogden, Utah, born January the eleventh, 1897, wanted the facts of history told upon the printed page. He wanted to see history written from fact, not from intuition or from deduction or from the argument *a priori* and the flowery heights of what he castigated as "the literary mind."

It all began, of course, with DeVoto's defense of the frontier and the frontiersman. Various writers, Van Wyck Brooks among them, had intimated that life on the American frontier possessed a certain aridity. To live there would stifle artistic talent in anybody, let alone in Samuel Clemens. The frontiersman was said to be crude, subsisting at a rudimentary animal level; his life lacked every good thing which civilization possesses. From Mormon to mountain trapper, the Westerners were nothing

more than transplanted Puritans, with the Puritan's hatred
of beauty, art, and love.

It was enough to make a Utah man shrink in his bones,
or burst the boundaries of Rocky Mountain profanity.
"The frontier is not a person," DeVoto retorted indignantly. "A historian does not speak of the frontier's tastes
and preferences. The historian sees the frontier as many
different places, in many different stages of development,
inhabited by many people with many different kinds and
degrees of culture, intelligence, racial tradition, family
training, and individual capacity. He cannot speak of the
life of the frontier, for he knows many kinds of frontiers
and many kinds of people living many kinds of lives." If
these literary historians would examine the facts, they
would discover, for one thing, that the American people
were "incurably musical. Working westward they carried
fiddles and a folk art. Catgut strings were an article of
commerce in the fur trade. . . . And there might be music
near the three Tetons in the country of the Blackfeet."

"We must be accurate," he said further. "We must
make our descriptions exact, verify our conclusions, we
must avoid certainty and the loaded dice. Metaphysics is
not experience and the philosophy of history is not history."

It infuriated DeVoto to have a so-called historian prefer
the *must be* and the *ought to be* to the cold fact. History is
not made by "thinking it out." Writers mistake "the quirks
of their own emotions for the contours of objective fact."
They write about the American mind, about Puritans or

the frontier without having studied America, Puritans, or
the frontiersman. "Authority is not born full grown," he
wrote, "in any mind, nor can any one come to it by staring
into his own soul, or at his navel, or into the high priest's
emerald breast-plate." DeVoto could not endure man-
made utopias, gospels, prophecies. He said he had had his
fill of them in his youth. "Absolutes," he wrote, "are a
mirage. And in my desert country, mirages are a com-
monplace." DeVoto, an expert on the religious sects that
blossomed in the American forties of the last century, was
at his ironic best when describing them. Always, when he
says the word Mormon, the pressure rises. "The Underwriters of Salvation," he called them. Mormonism was
"the most colorless of American heresies," and Zion, city
of the Saints, in the end "became a successful business ven-
ture, blended with the map and joined hands with the
damned."

Small wonder that Ogden, Utah, did not welcome its
native son on the few occasions when he returned there.
In boyhood, Benny must have been a difficult child, pre-
cocious, disconcertingly quick, disconcertingly inquisitive
and critical. In 1943, on my way east from Oregon, I
stopped off at Ogden to see what I could find about that
boy and that young man. (Even then, I wanted to write
about him.) DeVoto's Aunt Martha — Mrs. Grey — told
me that as a child, Benny was aloof. Not a country boy
by nature, but studious. His brilliant father, Florian, insisted that he study. Florian DeVoto, by the way, read
Latin and Greek for his entertainment until he died.

When Benny was four he could read *Hiawatha*. As a young man he was bored, his aunt said, if people talked about ordinary things. "Come down to earth," she used to tell him. "Just listen and be interested."

Before I went to Ogden I had read an early article of DeVoto's, published in the *American Mercury* when its author had not yet gone east to live. The piece opens with a discouraged tourist, descending from the Overland Limited at Ogden. I, too, stepped from that train and walked out of a station which DeVoto had called "hideous." I was confronted, as his tourist had been, with a wide flat street between ugly houses. And then I, too, looked up and saw, at either end of the street, the mountains, red, pink, yellow, and dusted with snow — mountains, DeVoto had written, "on which the gods of the Utes walked in the cool of the day."

The stories that I heard in Ogden were diverse. Some were mere gossip, all were amusing. As a child, it seems, Benny was beautiful — black-haired, with fine features; at the age of six he won a beauty contest. Then, said his Aunt Martha, he climbed on the roof and fell off and broke his nose. His friends and his enemies had been hospitable to me; one can have a good time in Ogden. But after three clear and pleasant days in the city and environs, I could see why it was that a man of intellect and imagination had to leave Ogden, had to climb onto the Overland Limited, head east, and shake the dust of Utah from his shoes. Yet I saw also how, for the rest of his life, no matter where that Ogden boy might travel, to the Ultima Thule or the seven radiant cities of Antilia, he could not forget those startling deep canyons, that mountain air, and the glowing peaks where walked the gods of the Utes. Born and raised among those dry hard mountains a man must live haunted, his life dedicated to recounting the story of that country and of the caravans which traveled to it from the East.

Bernard DeVoto lived with history, read history at night and in the morning, talked history, and was restless when other people did not want to talk history. When I began to write about John Adams, I asked DeVoto if I should buy the *Dictionary of American Biography*, known to historians as the D.A.B. There are twenty-one volumes and it is not cheap. DeVoto was surprised at my question and surprised that I did not already own the volumes. "Of course, buy it," he said. "It's good to read in bed at night before you go to sleep."

DeVoto lived with history and he lived with maps. I never saw such a man for maps. His last four books of history have maps for end papers; maps lined his study walls when he was working. In 1947, DeVoto came to stay with us in Bryn Mawr, Pennsylvania; he was to give a lecture on those doubtful historical characters, "The Welsh Indians." He arrived with a suitcase full of maps, big folded maps of the United States, mostly west of Council Bluffs, Iowa. He spread them on the floor of our living room and we crawled from map to map, with Benny talking, until our knees were sore and our minds enlarged with names like Ogallala, Little Blue, Three Forks, Elephant Butte, the country of the Mandans, the Arikaras, and the Blackfeet. When he left our house DeVoto gave us, as guest present, a beautiful book about maps. And he never ceased to urge upon me, to my great advantage, the study of maps — though during all those years I happened to be investigating not river, sea, and landfall but the geography of men's minds and the cosmography of their laws and constitutions.

DeVoto was generous to other writers — not a common trait among members of the union. When a manuscript needed editing he was ready with time and effort. And he was a believer in good editing; he knew there is more than one way to compose a sentence and that the right way may take some seeking. He did not spare those who came to him. The treatment was rough, and sensitive souls have been known to turn and flee at his approach. Yet he understood the writer's psychology, I think, as few men have understood it, although he declared that he seldom knew the right thing to say to authors. "They bleed on," he wrote, "from wounds healed long ago, which began by seeming mortal but turned out only to need a Band-aid or five pages of type."

Once DeVoto wrote a paragraph to me, about American history and his feeling toward it. (I have quoted this in my last book, but it's worth repetition.) The words came, remember, from a man tough-minded, who professed to write history from the facts and the facts alone. I was working, at the time, on our revolutionary period, and I had been challenged by a scholar who declared that my view of American history was too romantic altogether.

The men who composed our United States Constitution were interested not in ideals but in property — their own property and its protection. George Washington only went into the army to recover his lands along the Shenandoah, and so on. In distress I wrote DeVoto, telling my chagrin because I had not made adequate rebuttal. He wrote back at once. Here is what he said:

Sure you're romantic about American history. What your detractor left out of account was the fact that it is the most romantic of all histories. It began in myth and has developed through centuries of fairy stories. Whatever the time is in America it is always, at every moment, the mad and wayward hour when the prince is finding the little foot that alone fits into the slipper of glass. It is a little hard to know what romantic means to those who use the word umbrageously. But if the mad, impossible voyage of Columbus or Cartier or La Salle or Coronado or John Ledyard is not romantic, if the stars did not dance in the sky when our Constitutional Convention met, if Atlantis has any landscape stranger or the other side of the moon any lights or colors or shapes more unearthly than the customary homespun of Lincoln and the morning coat of Jackson, well, I don't know what romance is. Ours is a story mad with the impossible, it is by chaos out of dream, it began as dream and it has continued as dream down to the last headlines you read in a newspaper. And of our dream there are two things above all others to be said, that only madmen could have dreamed them or would have dared to — and that we have shown a considerable faculty for making them come true. The simplest truth you can ever write about our history will be charged and surcharged with romanticism, and if you are afraid of the word you had better start practising seriously on your fiddle.

The Writer

by
Edith R. Mirrielees

A FTER Bernard DeVoto's death, the editors of *Harper's Magazine* had letters from many readers of "The Easy Chair" expressing their grief and their sense of irreparable loss. Some of these they published, and in one of them the writer referred to "the revered DeVoto."

The phrase stuck in my mind for two reasons. First, of course, because it was so richly deserved. High talent, integrity, self-forgetful devotion to the common good as against individual greed or group stupidity — these are qualities that extort reverence. The second reason, though, was more personal. It was that nobody, nobody anywhere, would have laughed so loud and so long as would the subject himself at having the term "revered" applied to him. The several thousand of his letters now gathered in the DeVoto Collection at Stanford University give expression to nearly every emotion of which the human mind is capable. The one conspicuously lacking is self-satisfaction, whether satisfaction with himself as a person or satisfaction with his published performance.

Thank you, darling [this in answer to a letter of congratu-
lation] but "great" is not a word that attaches itself to any
work of mine.

I am not much of a person or an intelligence. I am pretty
close to being a former writer . . .

Any kind of offer could tempt me. On the proviso that
it would get me out of Cambridge . . . Every so often I
have to try the expedient, known to be delusive, of getting
to a place not filled with reminders of my failures and stimu-
lants to remember my protean baseness. Signs pile up that one
more such is at hand.

What sprinkled his letters with such self-derogations
was not mock modesty; anyone who knew him came soon
to know that. Partly they resulted from the depressions
which periodically overwhelmed him. Still more, they
came from a view of existence which perhaps may best be
named cosmic, one which displays the human being set
against the backdrop of the universe and there posturing
and proclaiming and complaining — a pinch of dust de-
manding the attention of the round world.

The letters, whatever their mood or subject, are pure
DeVoto throughout, pungent, forceful, exaggerative, hu-
morous, though with humor used often as an overlay for
pain. Especially to the four correspondents whom he
named in one letter "the only ones whose opinions I care
a damn about," his thoughts poured out on paper as freely
and as tumultuously as in talk. Handwritten pages, often
eight and ten of them to a letter, were filled with com-
ments on work in hand, summaries of work projected,
news of his family, himself, his acquaintances, the state
of the nation as he saw it, the state of the would-be serious

writer in that nation — all expressed with an intensity that puts the stamp "DeVoto" on every page.

In the whole collection a Boswell would find material worthy of his talents. Short of a Boswell, only full reproduction, supplemented by such editing as DeVoto himself gave to the *Lewis and Clark Journals,* could properly present them. All, then, a single article can do, if it can do that, is to bring back to some readers recollection of the excited expectation that a new "Easy Chair" or the appearance of a new book brought with it.

The paragraphs reproduced here are arranged not chronologically but by topic. The first deals with one crisis in a life that abounded in crises. In 1935, DeVoto, under strong urging, had undertaken the editing of *The Saturday Review.* The position, as he soon found, was miserably unsatisfactory, the *Review* on the rocks financially, its staff at odds with one another, the terms on which he had understood himself to be engaged (for example, that his summers should be free for writing) first disregarded, then denied. At the end of his second year he withdrew. "You will hear more of this," he promised one friend at the close of seven pages recounting the deceptions and frustrations which had surrounded him. By the time the "more" came, however, his earlier emotions had been pushed out by one still stronger — the emotion of sheer relief.

I am, considering the state of the world, anxious enough about my family, but convinced I can scrape along somehow. For the rest, I am ten years younger than when you last saw me. Considering my record, it may be foolish of me to hope that I can make myself over into a writer again. Nevertheless, I am acting on the hope.

All sorts of offers are being made to me; the publishers seem to agree with my one-time colleagues that I am a good writer. Some of the damnedest propositions that you ever heard. A centennial volume — a history of American literature (four publishers), a history of recent American literature (two publishers); a history of the United States (two publishers) — and so on, idiotic notions, especially to a man who wants to write his own books. But as yet no jobs. Except one that I may have to take. Lee Hartman wants me to reorganize the review column of *Harper's*.

"The job that I may have to take" led, of course, to "The Easy Chair," a chair he held for twenty years. "— twenty years of shooting my face off in *Harper's*. Twenty years of public folly." Twenty years, too, however, in which a nationwide clientele attached itself to those particular pages in that particular magazine.

In the same years his other writing went on steadily — a record, in amount as in quality, of an all but incredible industry. Industry, indeed, was the one virtue he now and then allowed himself.

I suppose I ought to list the current occupations. I'm finishing my fur trade book in first draft and beginning to revise the novel, which I hope to God you won't read. . . . I'm also writing a pamphlet — historical, polemical and hortatory — on censorship. I'm also preparing to write, for Mr. Luce and a sum in round numbers, four of them, an article on the detective story. That makes four jobs in what the physicists call a simultaneity.

. . . as age not creeps but gallops upon me, I work not less but more and this year have done more work, written more words, traveled more miles, and read more books, more damn books, than in any other period of the same length in my past. I seem to have been a softie up to now . . . this year I've been writing nights as well as mornings and afternoons. I can't see that I've done anything beyond poulticing my ego with professional pride, but anyway I've done that — and one result unlooked for has been to retire my depression to the sidelines. There has been no time for it to operate.

What "that" amounted to, aside from poulticing the ego and providing a temporary escape from depression, was clearer in readers' eyes than in his own. The letter was written in 1946. Between *The Saturday Review* fiasco of 1937 and the setting down of the paragraph just quoted had come *The Year of Decision* and *Across the Wide Missouri*, books that placed their writer in the top rank of living American historians.

Though in his own eyes he was still a "pro," a hack writer, employable for whatever task came to hand, he nonetheless recognized the pro's importance within his field, his sheer usefulness in a world growing daily more distraught.

Is there not something respectworthy in us hacks, the pro's who do the world's work in words while the poet and the literary and the geniuses secrete beauty and revel in the shimmering of their egos?

Respectworthy or not, let anyone disregard this particular pro, block his way to information, strive to mislead him, and all the waters of Ladore boiled down on the offender's head.

I went in there [a Washington office] a journalist on a white horse, and he cast his mantle around me and wept on my shoulder and gave me his calumet and welcomed me to the battle. Just fine! Only he lied and lied, and I knew he was lying and later proved it.

Seems I wasted another month in the Pentagon, wholly unable to persuade the War Department to let me do the job I'd been asked to do by the War Department. So, going broke and crazy in a dead heat, I came home leaving word that I'd come if called but not otherwise. I won't be called, so Guadalcanal, etc. is out. I told you I'd end up writing about the Civil War if any war. As Jim Boyd's hero put it, "God-damn me if I ever love another country — or try to serve one."

. . . As a family, we were about wiped out in the spring by a damned recurrent virus. Mine eased up enough for a week to allow me to go to Washington and save the nation some more . . .

Saving the nation some more was a lifetime preoccupation with him, especially the saving of the West, his love for which and hate of which existed in almost equal proportions.

The efforts of my native West to destroy itself forthwith are an even duller replay than the efforts of the East to keep it from doing so. We have been through this thing so often that there is little satisfaction in putting on the old costume and going out to play the roles that our grandfathers created. It's as stylized and as dreary as the D'Oyly Carte productions. I feel like Martyn Green singing the Lord Chancellor's part for the five thousandth time. . . . There is a moderate satisfaction in my Western mail, which invariably begins with the truism that I am a bastard and goes on to say, most awfully, that I have lost the Western friends I never had . . .

and in having the Communist label widely pinned on me as it has not been for a full ten years. I promise you not to surfeit with satisfaction.

Last week [this in 1950] I wrote an *Easy Chair* about 1794 for the sole purpose of reminding myself that the Republic is not unacquainted with desperation. I could quarrel with God in behalf of our generation for what He has seen fit to make us see. I have a sense of the nation's being swept off on the floodwaters of events as I've never had before. And we don't look too good — we never do in this stage of our troubles . . . While I was writing about 1794 I was yearning with a sorrowful tug for George Washington. Suddenly all the political genius of the world was in the United States. We could use some now.

So far as his letters show, DeVoto's first literary fascination — and, indeed, his lifelong one — seems to have been with fiction; the novel was his Old Man of the Sea, never to be wholly shaken off. In a long backward look, he estimates and describes what was his method with a very early attempt:

. . . whenever I reached a difficult passage, I pumped in purple ink and waded across it. Sometimes I wake up nights sweating and find that I've been remembering parts of that book.

. . . The horrid development is that I, who of all men should know better, seem to be drifting back to fiction. Socially, I judge, it is a good thing, for I shall bore even fewer than in my other departments, but I cannot account to myself for the shift. Fantasy may be the answer.

In the forties, the long prepared-for histories now realities, he writes:

I have committed another lapse of judgment. I'm a hundred pages into a novel, it seems I won't learn or at least won't heed. MOUNTAIN TIME was a resounding flop in all ways except sales — it sold 1500 copies, which is inconceivable for a book of mine! and 300,000 to the Dollar Book Club. I figure that, including me, exactly nine people liked it. We can count on that sum being at least halved by the new one . . . I don't even know if I'll like it.

On work partly completed he now and then asked the judgment of some writing friend, prefacing the asking with apologies and pointing out ways of escape:

> Another penalty of friendship is on its way to you. If you read it, you will see that what counts is that the roadblock has been broken. That is not worth reading time, and you are granted Lenten dispensation.
>
> You can stop it with a wire, postcard, or published prayer. If you don't stop it, in due time, say six or eight weeks, there will arrive at your desk a hunk of what purports to be fiction. Not, all things considered, a large hunk. Say, 50,000 words.
>
> I don't know why we do these things, but I know you will probably do it. I do too. I curse horribly and my soul corrugates but I do them. You are too much of a lady to curse, though I may caution you that many a soul has been damned by a darn, but you'll — smile and tell me you'd just love to and it is a great privilege. It's a great imposition and a hell of a bore. . . .

How many "great impositions" he himself endured is barely suggested in his letters. Mostly, he plowed patiently through whatever was sent him. Patience, though, breaks down with one repeater, who, persistently calling for help, also patronizes the helper.

There is a dear, sweet thing hereabouts whose entirely un-publishable mss I've been reading for fifteen years, a novelist, understand. I've always treasured what she said when she learned I'd finished my '36 book: "You must be very glad. Now you can go back to creative work." This is like gall-stones or a migraine that won't end.

As quotations from his letters have already shown, DeVoto's seemingly inexhaustible energy habitually de-manded more than one iron in the fire. His three histories of the West, and the *Lewis and Clark Journals* along with them are, in effect, one history — all stirring in the writer's mind through the same years; all dealing with the same tremendous theme; all except the *Journals* reaching back, even against their creator's conscious wish, into those earlier centuries which form a backdrop for the Western drama. In 1947, six years before the *Journals'* publica-tion, "The Lewis and Clark job stretches endlessly, and I may have to finish it in hell," and two years later,

I'm scared stiff. For lots of reasons. Never before have I worked so long and so minutely to prepare myself, and never have I known so comparatively little when I began to write, for you don't really prepare yourself, regardless, to write Three Centuries of World History, which in the lowest mo-ments seems to be what I've got to do. Again, I have this time a big, even a great and majestic theme by the tail, and who am I to go chasing after great themes? This will be the loud-est flop since the tower of Babel fell.

... what annoys me is that so objective — well, that's what we gravely say — a thing as history should have its processes so deep and hidden in the unconscious. I had written — be-cause it turned out I must — almost exactly 100,000 words when I reached the place where I originally thought the thing began. And all of it different from what I supposed I'd do — from what I like to do. I like small periods of time — this one deals in detail with two centuries, and just for the hell of it drops back to 700 A.D. and back of that to the ice age. I like to do personalities; most of the names in this one get less than a paragraph. I write American history, I tell people, but this is the expansion and transformation of Europe . . . And so on. No one has ever been so surprised.

The paragraph above, written in 1950, was provoked by the comment, already quoted, of that "dear, sweet thing" who for years had despatched for DeVoto's reading her worthless attempts at fiction. Sweet and silly and immeasurably presumptuous — yes. But a reluctant vote of thanks is due her nonetheless for having brought the passage into being. Nowhere is set down more succinctly the tremendous backlog of labor, the compulsions not of his own making, out of which the DeVoto histories came.

The Citizen

by
Arthur M. Schlesinger, Jr.

Bernard DeVoto was born in Ogden, Utah, in 1897 of a Mormon-Catholic marriage. These facts are crucial to an understanding of his subsequent career.

Birth made him a westerner. It gave him an identification with the experience of the frontier and a permanent concern with the process by which America became a continental nation. It also made him a Populist. I recognize that this term has gone out of fashion; but, as DeVoto used it, it was an honorable word. It meant a belief that the basic conflict in America was among sections rather than among classes. It meant a broad sympathy for the pioneer over the capitalist — for the men who opened up and settled a region as against those who came along later and drained it of its wealth. It meant an abiding, if sometimes sorely tried, faith in the good sense of plain Americans. It meant a conviction that people ought to leave the world a better place than they found it.

If environment thus made him a westerner and Populist, the Mormon-Catholic collision in his parentage made him a relativist and a skeptic. He was, so to speak, suspended in his own family between two revelations, authoritatively certified as divine but mutually contradictory. His boyhood intensified the puzzlement of this clash. His first education was in the pieties of a convent school; at the same time, he lived among people sworn to an incompatible creed and no less persuaded that theirs was the unique road to salvation. This experience bred in him a profound mistrust of revelation in general. "I early acquired," he later wrote:

> a notion that all gospels were false, and all my experience since then has confirmed it. All my life people around me have been seeing a Light, that, with a vision certified as excellent by the best oculists, I have been unable to see. At first astonishing contradictions in the reports they gave me troubled my mind, but, you well understand, I came to conclude that absolutes were a mirage. And in my desert country, mirages are also commonplace.[1]

His upbringing thus defined the poles of activism and skepticism — of passion and detachment — between which he oscillated most of his life. From an early age he had a nonconformist's love of freedom, a Populist's rage at injustice, and, though he would have indignantly denied it, a crusader's desire to knock sense into people's heads and build a better world. And from an early age he also had a relativist's dislike of all forms of dogma and revelation and a pragmatist's distrust for all varieties of ideologist and prophet. These two divergent strains warred within him

[1] *Minority Report* (Boston: Little, Brown, 1940), 164–65.

until in the last years of his life he fused them into an effective synthesis.

The inner tension is visible from his first days in college. As a freshman at the University of Utah, he was a crusader. He helped found a chapter of the Inter-collegiate Socialist Society, he backed faculty members under criticism for heterodox views, and, when the university disbanded the Society and fired the professors, he felt the Salt Lake City campus was no place for him. The next year he transferred to Harvard. Here evangelism gave way to empiricism, and he devoted himself to science — to positive knowledge, in other words, as the best answer to the pretensions of dogma and revelation.

His first ambition was to become a mineralogist. But, though he got through geology and chemistry well enough, he encountered difficulties with crystallography. He learned the structure of crystals from textbook models, but he was never able to match these ideal crystals with the "wrenched, distorted, displaced, reversed, bent, crushed, and completely transformed crystals of actual rock."[2] This experience only confirmed his doubts about the infallibility of theories and his preference for existence over essence. The defeat by crystallography did not, however, diminish his fascination with science, and he found a more congenial outlet in psychopathology. Soon he planned to go to medical school and become a doctor. Then the American entrance into the First World War interrupted his plans. When he returned to Harvard after

[2] *Minority Report*, 172–73.

two years in the Army, he believed himself too old and too broke for a medical career.[3] But the ideal of the doctor cast a spell over him for the rest of his life; on the whole, doctors seemed to him of all people to have best united disinterested analysis and beneficial result, to have best resolved his own tormenting split between the scientist and the reformer.

The war had meanwhile offered a new challenge to his crusading impulse. He regarded Wilson's decision of 1917 as just and necessary; and he promptly volunteered for the Army. His skill as a marksman meant that he saw service as a rifle instructor in the United States rather than as a soldier in France, but he endured the dreary months without losing faith in the war's essential idealism. Still determined to make the world safe for democracy back in Ogden after the war, he joined the American Legion and tried to use it to help elect a liberal lawyer to the state legislature. In 1920 he campaigned for James M. Cox, Franklin D. Roosevelt, and the League of Nations.

The '20's were for DeVoto, as for most Americans, a vacation from public policy. He was busy establishing himself as a teacher of English at Northwestern: busy soon in marrying the prettiest freshman in his class; busy too in beginning his career as a writer. As a reformer, he wrote about education; as a skeptic, he sent his reforming pieces to the *American Mercury*. By 1927 he was doing well enough to abandon Evanston and attempt a life as a free-lance writer. Attracted by the Harvard University Library, he moved back to Cambridge.

[3] *Minority Report*, 173.

The DeVoto who came to Cambridge was still at heart the western radical. An impassioned essay in *Harper's* in 1934 called "The Plundered Province" brought up to date the Populist version of the history of the West. In language that would have delighted James B. Weaver, DeVoto described the procession of marauders who had pillaged his native land; the mines and the railroads; then the water companies, the road companies, the land companies, the grain-storage companies, the mortgage companies, the banks: "all of them looted the country in utter security with the Government itself guaranteeing them against retributive action by the despoiled." As a consequence, "the few alpine forests of the West were levelled, its minerals were mined and smelted, all its resources were drained off through the perfectly engineered gutters of a system designed to flow eastward. It may be empire-building. The westerner may be excused if it has looked to him like simple plunder."

But this was not all. "Besides taking over the country, then, the East added direct usury." Through the entire West, said DeVoto, "no one has ever been able to borrow money or make a shipment or set a price except at the discretion of a board of directors in the East, whose only interest was to sequester Western property as an accessory of another section's finance." Of course, a part of the loot had flowed back to the West through the redistributive effect of federal taxation; but this was only a sort of bakshish; "the West has sometimes been tipped a fractional per cent of its annual tribute in the form of Government works or social supervision." Moreover, even this had been dispensed to the accompaniment of eastern complaints about the mendicant West and only as an expedient to buy off the farmers when they grew troublesome. And the result of eastern exploitation? The West, wrote DeVoto, "is the one section of the country in which bankruptcy, both actuarial and absolute, has been the determining condition from the start."[4]

"The Plundered Province" is notable as evidence of DeVoto's continuing populism. It is also notable as one of the few sustained pieces he wrote about the West during these first years in Cambridge. It did not precisely exhaust his radicalism: when he became editor of the *Harvard Graduates' Magazine* in 1930, he enlivened the first numbers of this previously sedate journal with attacks on the Watch and Ward Society for its censorship of books and on Harvard's new House system as a possible institutionalization of Ivy League snobbery. Yet his radicalism now observed distinct limits — limits displayed, for example, in his attitude toward the Sacco-Vanzetti case.

Sacco and Vanzetti had gone to the electric chair in Charlestown in the very month in 1927 in which DeVoto arrived in Cambridge. DeVoto had no doubt about the reasons: "two humble Italians were executed because the ruling class did not like their political beliefs." But the totality of his reaction suggests the extent to which in this period radicalism was subdued by relativism. "Several inabilities," as he put it in 1932, "cut me off from my fraternal deplorers of this judicial murder." Most of all, "I was unable to feel surprise at the miscarriage of justice

[4] *Forays and Rebuttals* (Boston: Little, Brown, 1936), 53–57.

— unable to recall any system of society that had pre-
vented it or to imagine any that would prevent it."[5] His
best novel, *We Accept with Pleasure* (1934), effectively
conveys this mixture of indignation and acquiescence. The
vivid picture in the novel of Boston on the night of the
execution testified to DeVoto's sense of the crime against
justice. Yet the work left a final impression, in the words
of Garret Mattingly, of "the impermanence and futility
of the emotions aroused, and the inexorable impersonality
of the historical process at work."[6]

Increasingly, acquiescence seemed to be triumphing
over indignation. By 1936 DeVoto, in the preface to his
first collection of essays, *Forays and Rebuttals,* appeared
ready to bid an explicit farewell to liberal illusion. Ten
years ago, he said, he had been all for reform, but,

> like all reformers, I outrageously oversimplified the problem.
> Today I know a good deal more . . . I know that most pro-
> posed reforms are undesirable, and that practically all of them
> are impossible of achievement and must produce conditions
> worse than the diseases they undertake to cure."[7]

He was speaking specifically of educational reform, but
his remarks had a wider application. After 1932 his essays,
in Mr. Mattingly's succinct description, were "full of ridi-
cule of planned societies and Marxist dialectics, and usually
assume the complete futility of trying to reform anything."[8]

---

[5] Garrett Mattingly, *Bernard DeVoto: A Preliminary Appraisal* (Boston:
Little, Brown, 1938), 35–36.
[6] Mattingly, *DeVoto*, 35–36.
[7] *Forays*, ix.
[8] Mattingly, *DeVoto*, 55.

How is one to account for this apparent swing to the political right, especially at a time when in the nation liberalism, after years in the wilderness, had gained exuberant control of political power? Actually, of course, these two phenomena, far from being contradictory, were intimately related. DeVoto's nonconformist instincts always led him to run against the popular grain. The passion to correct the fashionable errors of the day led him inevitably during the high noon of the New Deal to turn his fire on the excesses of liberalism. He could do this the more easily because he was developing a theory of liberalism which identified the reforming mind, not with pragmatism and experiment, but with *a priori* ideology.

He reached this identification by analogies from the literary scene. As editor of the *Saturday Review of Literature* in the mid-'30's, he made it his office to champion pluralism and relativism against all absolutes. The "literary mind" became his particular target. It was characterized, he believed, by an incorrigible preference for generalizations over facts. To erect "articulated structures of abstractions as a rampart against experience" might provide comfort and reassurance; but "the theory killeth."[9]

He objected, for example, to literary historians who, as he saw it, were rewriting the past in terms of their own preconceptions.

> All these literary efforts display a hunger for unity. They are efforts to impose order and simplicity upon an obstinate

[9] *Minority Report*, 161.

multiplicity, and their authors are incorrigible monists . . . There is an eternal, fundamental and irreconcilable difference between fantasy, any kind of fantasy, and fact. The fantasies of the literary historian are frequently beautiful and nearly always praiseworthy, but they are a form of protective or wishful thinking, a form of illusion and even of delusion, and they must be constantly denounced as such.[10]

He found it easy to move from the literary mind to the reforming mind.

My sense of propriety becomes active [DeVoto wrote in 1937] when they take over that twelve-inch rod, which does not exist, apply it as a measuring rod to things that do exist — and then as a result of those measurements order me to believe and behave in specified ways, order a novelist or a poet to write books in specified ways or else, and order society to reconstruct itself according to syllogisms . . . Idealism, whether moral or metaphysical or literary, may be defined as a cross-lots path to the psychopathic ward, Berchtesgaden, and St. Bartholomew's Eve. Absolute means absolutism.[11]

Marxism, of course, was the supreme absolutism in politics; and he wrote brilliantly and devastingly about the delusions of the Communists, the fellow travelers and the Popular Fronters. But even liberal reform seemed to him almost as susceptible to the intoxication of abstractions.

All this was crystallized in his mind by a new friendship in Cambridge. He had come to know L. J. Henderson, a formidable member of the Harvard faculty, noted for his pink whiskers and his powerful intelligence. Henderson

[10] *Forays*, 168, 177–78.
[11] *Minority Report*, 184.

had been trained as a doctor and had made his reputation as a biological chemist; he thus satisfied DeVoto's admiration for the medical scientist. In more recent years his interest had begun to shift from science to society. Henderson was a type unusual in America; he was an exceedingly intelligent and articulate conservative; and his innate conservatism had been reinforced by his immersion in the writings of the Italian sociologist Vilfredo Pareto. When Henderson introduced DeVoto to Pareto, DeVoto found what seemed for a moment perfect allies in his battle against the intellectuals, whether literary or political, who were bemused by abstractions. In a piece in the *Saturday Review of Literature* in 1933, DeVoto seemed almost to herald Pareto as the prophet of a new revelation. Under the spell of Pareto he could write, for example, in 1934, "Socially, it is much better for any writer (or any realtor, farmer, or stevedore) to increase his sense of personal integrity by identifying himself with a group than it is for him to suffer impairment in that sentiment by remaining just an individual."[12]

But DeVoto was far too intractable an individualist to stay very long in so self-abnegating a mood. By 1937 he wrote disarmingly, "I am not much of a Paretian." He asked people to forget his *Saturday Review* piece of 1933 — "one of my unfortunate attempts to annoy certain literary people" — and concluded of the experience, "Though I learned much from Pareto, I was never a member of the movement but only a kind of cooperating press

[12] *Forays,* 320.

agent."[13] This is fair enough. After all, DeVoto did learn a good deal from Pareto, as well as from Henderson, and there was much anyone could profitably learn from both. For DeVoto the effect was to strengthen his skepticism at the expense of his radicalism and to exaggerate for a season his disdain for reform.

All this shaped his reaction to the New Deal. His first attitude was one of wary approval. The main New Deal policies did little to offend his sense of propriety. His knowledge of the frontier, for example, divested him of any illusions about the sanctity of American individualism. "The very conditions of frontier life in the desert imposed cooperation,"[14] he wrote; and again, "To the dismay of bond-holders and cartoonists, the West is integrated collectively. It will stay that way while climate is climate. That also may be a portent for the nation whose dream has receded."[15]

He was also grateful to the New Deal for the absence of social disorder. "Considering the gravity of the situation, the appeal to violence has been shockingly small — and un-American. During the worst of 1932 one saw miserable 'Hoovervilles' built sometimes literally in the shadow of elevators and mills bursting with grain and flour that could not be sold — and none of the wretched seized the food. To a historian it is all but incredible."[16]

He praised TVA, SEC, and New Deal policies in agri-

13 *Minority Report,* 167, 180.
14 *Forays,* 42–43.
15 *Forays,* 64.
16 "Notes on the American Way," *Harper's,* May 1938.

culture, labor, conservation, and relief. No one paid a
more stirring tribute to the Writers' Project established
under the Works Progress Administration and its splendid
series of state guides.[17] He voted for Roosevelt in 1932
and again in 1936. But he objected, with increasing vehemence, to what he regarded as the seizure of the New
Deal by the ideologists — by those who felt they knew
better than the ordinary man what was good for him. His
objections finally boiled over in 1937 when Roosevelt
followed the attempt to enlarge the Supreme Court by
proposals for the reorganization of the executive branch
of the government.

DeVoto obviously did not regard "Desertion from the
New Deal" as a definitive statement; he never republished
it, for example, in his collection of essays. But it registered
sharply his mood of the day. He had been willing to go
along with the New Deal for a long time, he wrote, despite the "hooey and hosannas," the "fruitless experiments
and ghastly waste," the "immensely multiplied bureauc-
racy . . . dreadful increase of expenditure . . . centralization of demagogic control." All these things constituted
a steep price, but they were all in the legitimate bill, "and
we were willing to pay it . . . We stood, and we found an
Administration that stood, for human interests above property interests. We accepted the implications, all of them,
and we wanted everything done that could be done."
But these latest proposals were too much. Oddly enough,
it was Roosevelt's relatively innocuous bills for govern-

17 "The Writers' Project," *Harper's*, January 1942.

ment reorganization that forced DeVoto over the brink. These bills, DeVoto declared, "proved what the Supreme Court bill had intimated: that the first Roosevelt Administration had been abandoned, that the President now thought he could do the impossible, and that he wasn't concerned about what happens when you try to do the impossible and fail." These bills, he added, "assume that our present form of government is ineffective and played out . . . that we are on the brink of dissolution and armed revolt . . . that you can change social energies with a wave of a hand and regenerate the human race with tricks and some centralization." The New Deal had "sold out to the millenial vision"; "the liberal government dies of an overdose of idealism, arrogance, and miracles." Far from being the Kerensky of the American Revolution, Roosevelt had become its Trotsky, sacrificing everything on the altar of ideology.[18] Nor was this a passing mood. Six months later DeVoto described the New Deal as "clearly designed not to regulate the system of profits . . . but to transform it." He denounced deficit spending, derided the notion of a hundred billion dollar national income, and predicted inflation.[19] Writing in 1938, Garrett Mattingly could say, "Although Mr. Edmund Wilson was too intelligent, too sensitive to nuances, to class DeVoto as a right-winger, *Forays and Rebuttals* [a collection of DeVoto's magazine pieces] gives him some excuse to do so."[20]

Edmund Wilson was right: it was not that simple. Re-

[18] "Desertion from the New Deal," *Harper's*, October 1937.
[19] "The Game and the Candle," *Harper's*, March 1938.
[20] Mattingly, *DeVoto*, 55.

sponding to Wilson's challenge, DeVoto said, "I am, if you must have words, a pluralist, a relativist, an empiricist . . . We must avoid certainty, unity, vision and the loaded dice."[21] Such attitudes made him seem conservative only when he was confronting the liberals; when he started to confront the conservatives, these same attitudes made him recoil to the left. In 1940 he voted again, not without misgivings, for Roosevelt and the New Deal. The misgivings were due to Roosevelt's methods — his weakness for tricks and ruses, his unwillingness to take the people into his confidence. "There is no way of unifying a nation," De Voto warned, "by stealth, cunning, or sleight of hand . . . You assume that it is adult, intelligent, and courageous. You move openly and in the light of day, and you tell the truth." But he voted for Roosevelt nonetheless, because he approved the historic function of the Democratic party — "the fact that it has periodically been used by the forces in American democracy which permit the accomplishment of revolutionary ends peacefully and within the framework of our political institutions." In 1800, 1828, 1884, 1912, and 1932, he said, "the Democratic Party came to power charged with the duty of repairing situations and arresting trends which had carried the nation dangerously out of equilibrium . . . Five times a campaign charged it with what amounted to a revolution. Each time it accomplished the revolution. Each time its success proved the ability of the American system to rectify abuses in an orderly, peaceable, and democratic manner."[22] This state-

21 *Minority Report*, 165, 168.
22 "The Mugwump on November 6th," *Harper's,* January 1941.

ment more or less summed up his eventual position on the
New Deal. He wrote in his 25th Anniversary Report in
1943, "Politically, I am a New Dealer on Election Day
and a critic of the New Deal at other times. My social
ideas are a good deal left of the New Deal." And shortly
before his death in 1955:

> I doubt if anyone was ever a 100 per cent New Dealer —
> obviously Mr. Roosevelt wasn't — but, though many New
> Deal intellectuals had a much higher proof than mine, on the
> whole I had to go along. I got to that position by studying
> history, and the study of history has held me to the working
> principles of American liberalism.[23]

Even as he was pondering the choice in 1940, new
forces were beginning to dissolve his apparent conservatism of the mid-'30's. The retreat of the New Deal and
the revival of conservatism was unquestionably one factor; as always, DeVoto reoriented himself to oppose
new tides of fashion. Another factor was the resurgence
of his interest in the West. During most of the '30's,
he had been preoccupied with literature; but history was
reasserting itself in his inner imagination; and by the
end of the decade his great trilogy of westward expansion was beginning to take shape in his mind. In 1940,
preparing to write *The Year of Decision*, he made a long
automobile trip through the West. I had the good fortune to be his companion during a part of this journey.
I learned a great deal from him, and I saw renew within
him the concern with land and water and resources which

23 *The Easy Chair* (Boston: Houghton Mifflin, 1955), 9.

had more or less lain dormant since "The Plundered Province" in 1934.

As the conservationist hope now began to repossess him, there began to emerge in his mind a new and more appealing image of the liberal reformer. In the stress of the '30's, he had tended to see the reformer only as a doctrinaire obsessed with ideology. Yet a theoretical alternative remained: in 1937 he had allowed that "liberal" might refer to "people who try to apply logical and experimental knowledge to social problems" (while adding that this was quite separate from the usage of the day).[24] Now conservation offered the liberal an opportunity to re-emerge in this more benign light. DeVoto began to see the reformer not as ideological but as pragmatic. He saw him particularly, indeed, in the model of John Wesley Powell, the great director of the Geological Survey and the founder of modern conservation, whom DeVoto rediscovered with passion at the end of the decade. In his book of 1944, *The Literary Fallacy*, it was, above all, Powell whom DeVoto invoked as the means of rebuking the abstractionism of "the literary mind."

Powell had "a vision of society," said DeVoto, but he was no visionary. His vision was not composed out of abstract logic and beautiful thought; it was based on knowledge, rigorously determined, rigorously applied. Such a vision might legitimately serve as a basis for reform. Powell thus "conceived that society itself must be responsible for the preservation and development of their

[24] *Minority Report*, 111.

[natural] wealth" and fought "heroically" for this conception "against the forces of private exploitation, confused state and national interests, scandal, libel, and the ruthless drive of industry and finance."[25]

This was a significant tribute, for it was, after all, a tribute to a reformer, not to a hero out of Pareto or Henderson. As DeVoto's friend Wallace Stegner put it in his life of Powell (for which DeVoto wrote the introduction), Powell had "repudiated that reading of Darwinism which made man the pawn of evolutionary forces. In his view, man escaped the prison in which all other life was held, because he could apply intelligence and will to his environment and bend it."[26] There now surged within DeVoto a new determination to help fulfill John Wesley Powell's vision — in his words of 1944, "to make the land live rather than die, to build a society that may have decent security and dignity in accord with the conditions set by nature, to correct folly and restore social health."[27] The return to the West thus helped liberate him from the social quietism which had weighed upon him in the '30's.

Another factor, perhaps even more important, speeded the renewal of his radical idealism. This was the oncoming of the Second World War. Nothing does greater credit to DeVoto's intelligence than the clarity with which he saw the meaning of fascism. His character and concerns — his absorbing interest in the American past, his refusal ever

[25] *The Literary Fallacy* (Boston: Little, Brown, 1944), 128, 134–135.
[26] Wallace Stegner, *Beyond the Hundredth Meridian* (Boston: Houghton Mifflin, 1954), vii.
[27] "The Easy Chair," *Harper's*, February 1944.

to travel outside the American continent, his impatience with European examples and analogies — might well have predisposed him toward isolationism. But he had no doubt from the start either about American stakes in the war or about American responsibilities to the world. He had never surrendered to revisionist interpretations of the First World War, and he believed that German aggression offered a greater threat in 1939 than in 1914. Shortly after war broke out in 1939 he wrote, "We are in the war to stay. Whether formally remote or raising such armies as I was discharged from twenty-one years ago, we shall finish it — America will wage the war in one way or another and take the responsibility of fitting together what fragments of the world are left when it is finished."[28] The onset of war released the idealism which DeVoto had suppressed during the '30's. What of the young man who faced military service? "He will not grow up in the America he was born in," DeVoto wrote, "but neither did I or anyone else who has ever lived here; and if he cannot have the hope perhaps he can have the will to do more than I did in the shaping of his own America."[29]

War overshadowed our trip to the West in 1940. I can remember hot arguments in the editorial chambers of the then isolationist *Post-Dispatch* in St. Louis, as we tried to convince Fitzpatrick, Irving Dilliard, and the others that they should pay more attention to the Nazi rush across the Low Countries. Benny used to say afterward

[28] *Minority Report*, 132.
[29] *Minority Report*, 134–35.

that the *Post-Dispatch* published an editorial, reprinted up
and down the Mississippi Valley, warning the West against
panic-spreaders and warmongers from the East. I remember too when we drove up at the side of the road at sunset
outside Trinidad, Colorado, to hear Roosevelt's Fireside
Chat of May 26, 1940, on national defense. The red light
was fading on the Spanish Peaks; soon dusk fell, and everything was dark and silent and limitless. As Benny told the
story in a subsequent "Easy Chair": "Some Mexicans came
out of a little adobe hut, bowing, smiling, apologetic, and
asked if they might listen too. When it was finished one
of our guests said, 'I guess maybe America declare war
pretty soon now.' We waved goodbye and drove on to
Trinidad. I guess maybe." He wrote from New Mexico
in June:

> We have come twenty-five hundred miles, from Cambridge
> to Santa Fé. It is a dreamlike time for traveling across Amer-
> ica, with the fears loosed from the cave and the whole
> country roused to dread; and yet as we moved westward we
> found it progressively less roused, so that we have been
> bearers of evil tidings, the wave following behind us down
> the sun's path.[30]

In that eerie twilight period between the invasion of
Poland and Pearl Harbor, DeVoto never faltered in the
trenchancy of his perceptions. "What ought they to say?"
he wrote of the presidential candidates in November 1940.
"Simple, elementary, readily understandable things . . .

[30] "Letter from Santa Fé," *Harper's*, August 1940.

Just that the world is on fire. That America will be burned up unless you come awake and do something." When isolationists accused DeVoto of hysteria, he was able to turn back the charge: "Hysteria, remember, is the mind's retreat from what it dare not face. That's what happened to you, that's why your home town is serene. Of course you're quiet: anyone is quiet who is scared stiff. There is such a thing as coma."[31]

His piece of May 1941, "What to Tell the Young," provoked the heaviest mail he ever received in his life from a single article, heavier than in the worst days of the McCarthy fight. He asked the young men's question: "Would you send me out to die?" and answered: "When the time comes, yes . . . The chance for anyone is precarious but he must take it . . . What happens if he does not take the chance? In what terms will there be ambition, career, or individual significance if the United States goes down?"[32] When the young wrote back to say that they would be glad to fight if only they had a faith to defend, DeVoto was moved to wrath:

> You haven't got any faith, any belief? What you mean is that, in spite of all the chaos and waste of these years, even those of you who have had to work in a rich man's club have fed on fat so thick, have found life in America so soft, so promising, and so firmly established on the democratic assumptions that you have never been forced to take thought of it.
>
> You are forced to take thought of it now. The simple thing on which everything rests is endangered. It is not an

[31] "All Quiet along the Huron," *Harper's*, November 1940.
[32] "What to Tell the Young," *Harper's*, May 1941.

ordinance of Almighty God; it is only the labor of Americans. It can survive or it can go under; it can be forfeited or it can be fought for. Maintaining it long enough for you to voice your ignorance of it while you share and inherit it has sometimes required Americans to die for it who were quite as valuable to America as you are. What are you going to do about it?[33]

For DeVoto, the Civil War was the paradigm of all wars. It was the war he knew best, which preoccupied him most, and from which he drew images and arguments and parallels most freely. The impact of the Second World War on him can be measured by the change it wrought in the way he thought about the Civil War. In 1937, during his retreat from idealism, he had come almost to accept the revisionist view of the Civil War as a needless conflict brought about by "the humanitarians, the pure in heart, the idealists, and the dreamers." Nearly everyone lost the war, he said, "especially the American Republic." "So maybe the craven thing in 1860 would have turned out to be the best thing by 1937"; "maybe the best thing to have done was to hold on somehow, to give here and take there, to compromise when possible and yield when compromise failed, to do the next best thing no matter how little of the long view or the austere vision it had — but to insist on the established forms, maintain the accustomed mechanism, allay as much passion as might be and reduce as much friction, give the thing space to writhe in, and above all gain time."[34] This was a good piece of Paretianism, and in 1937 it might have seemed a tolerable formula. But when

---

[33] "Either-Or," *Harper's*, August 1941.
[34] *Minority Report*, 29–30.

Neville Chamberlain applied it at Munich in 1938, it began to lose its allure. By 1941 DeVoto had come to the position which he so brilliantly expounded in his destruction of the revisionist position after the war — that "the war had to be fought for many sufficient reasons . . . and the victory of the North was good for the modern world." Slavery, after all, was an evil; the South, in defending slavery, had "set itself square against the current of the democracy"; and the experience taught the nation "that some questions can be settled forever by war and that it is best to have them settled in your interest."[35]

Between them, the West and the war, aided by the fading away of the New Deal, emancipated DeVoto from Pareto and Henderson and permitted his radical idealism to come again to the fore. But his idealism now operated freely within the context of relativism and skepticism, and derived added force from that context. One began to feel that the two strains in DeVoto were no longer in conflict with each other: his empiricism was no longer hamstringing his populism; the two were working together to fulfill chosen purposes. John Wesley Powell helped point the way to reconciliation; so too in retrospect did Franklin Roosevelt, in whom DeVoto now began to recognize much the same union of pragmatism and idealism which was coming into balance in himself. In 1944 DeVoto voted a fourth time for Roosevelt. A year later, when the war came to its final end, he noted with regret that on the day of final victory, "No one, so far as I am

[35] "Easy Steps for Little Feet," *Harper's*, March 1941.

aware, spoke from Hyde Park to remind you that the man buried there had not lived to see this day and that his voice could not commemorate it by any miracle of radio."[36]

He thus entered the postwar world with idealism and skepticism, radicalism and relativism, in fruitful equilibrium. The nation's drift to the right in these years, working on DeVoto's natural contracyclical impulses, sharpened the edge of his radicalism. The hothouse attempt to construct a New Conservatism roused him to derision: "I feel no impulse to regress to Burke, Hobbes, Mandeville, or personal revelation."[37] The man for whom he felt the closest moral and intellectual sympathy was Elmer Davis, who combined, as he did, skepticism and radicalism in pungent union. His mission as scourge of the fashionable clichés now despatched him to the left rather than to the right of the reigning orthodoxies. This new position seemed more congenial to his temperament and his convictions: he was never freer than in this last period and never more productive.

He defined his political position in 1950: "I am a half Mugwump, 60 per cent New Dealer, 90 per cent Populist dirt-roads historian."[38] From this perspective he spoke out vigorously against tendencies toward smugness and conformity in the postwar world. In 1946 he turned sharply against the Truman Administration, pronouncing it "Republican in everything except the label." He found it hard for the moment "to determine which party Mr.

[36] "The Knowledge of Triumph," *Harper's*, October 1945.
[37] *Easy Chair*, 9.
[38] *Easy Chair*, 192.

Truman himself belongs to, but, when you cast the average of his policies, provided that is the right word, he seems to be playing about a yard back of the line on the Republican team, in the slot between tackle and end." Given this situation, DeVoto himself, like many Massachusetts liberals, cast his ballot for Henry Cabot Lodge, Jr., for senator against David I. Walsh. "I'm voting Republican," he said; adding quickly, "For this date and train only. It comes hard." He concluded about the election, " 'Business' has been given and has accepted its chance to run the United States. A lot of us think this is the last chance that Business will ever get and from where I sit it looks as if it has fumbled the ball on fourth down."[39] By the fall of 1948, DeVoto looked more genially on Truman and cast a relatively enthusiastic vote for his re-election.

But politics constituted only a minor part of DeVoto's postwar commentary. As society grew steadily more conservative, he found himself forced, in order to maintain the social equilibrium, to grow steadily more radical. An essay of 1952, called "The Third Floor," took off from the fact that old houses in Boston and Cambridge often had unheated third floors for the Irish servants who presumably did not need to be warm in winter. The people who had lived in comfort on the first and second floors, DeVoto reported, were now expressing indignation over the new affluence descending on the once poor and submissive people upstairs. Social Security, as DeVoto paraphrased the standard conservative complaint, "has

39 "The Easy Chair," *Harper's*, December 1946.

killed self-reliance and initiative. It has poisoned us; the United States is 'apparently so prosperous but is so rotten at the core. The five-day week and forty-hour week will cause our downfall' . . . now everyone is recklessly spending money." DeVoto went on to condemn "the idea that it is reckless to spend money you have earned but admirable to spend money someone else has earned, that a gentlewoman may properly tour the Orient on an inherited income but a waitress is bringing about our downfall if she buys a radio."[40]

But he was by no means uncritical of what his friend J. K. Galbraith would call the "affluent society." DeVoto long preceded contemporary critics of planned obsolescence and the style racket in his attack on the designed waste of postwar manufacturing: the tires that wore out after two thousand miles, the meat knives that could hardly cut butter, the appliances which cost more in maintenance than in original purchase. In the '30's, he had thought it important to defend the profit motive against what he regarded as the planning mania in Washington; the quest for profit at least kept things close to practical experience. But now that the acquisitive impulse was no longer contained by a liberal government, DeVoto was quick to denounce its excesses. Perhaps nothing was more symptomatic than his willingness now to criticize the profession which had so long been his ideal of humane and disinterested wisdom — the doctors. He still insisted that "the medical researcher and experimenter, while working

[40] *Easy Chair*, 34-35, 37.

at his trade, is just about the most admirable of human beings," but as an interest group, the profession seemed to him "biased, obscurantist, and reactionary to an astonishing degree." He contrasted the open mind the doctor showed in his laboratory with the "scarcity of objective thought, ignorance of economic and social developments, neophobia, docile acceptance of the fuehrer principle" he showed as a member of the American Medical Association and argued strongly for a national health program free of AMA interference or supervision.[41]

As against the affluent society, its avalanche of gadgets and gimmicks, its conviction that anything which made a profit justified itself and anything which didn't invited suspicion, DeVoto sought always to urge the indispensable importance of the free individual. And this meant for him, more forcibly than ever before, *all* individuals. The problems of the South, he wrote before the war had ended, including "the Negro problem (and Miss Lillian Smith of Clayton, Georgia, has pointedly reminded us all that we had better say the white problem)," were not the "private business" of southerners. "They are our business too. They are national problems. Everything that happens to you because of them happens to us as well." He recalled the 1850's — "racial myth, biological and ethnological dogma not only of white supremacy but of Southern superiority, suppression of civil rights . . . mobbing and lynching of people who dared to invoke the right to inquire, quarantine of the Southern mind." These were

[41] *Easy Chair*, 92–93, 101.

alarming enough in the 1850's, he said, and now that we have them in sharp contemporary perspective, they could be alarming again.[42] And he was appalled by the spread of southern folkways northward. Traveling across Wisconsin by train a year later, he heard middle westerners talking about "niggers" raping "eight or ten white women a day in Chicago." "For half an hour," DeVoto wrote, "I listened to a conversation which I would have said could not take place in Wisconsin in any circumstance whatever ... I think it was the most shocking experience I have ever had in a railroad car."[43] It would not have shocked L. J. Henderson, but DeVoto had moved far beyond the acquiescences of the '30's.

His most spectacular defense of the individual came, however, in the field of civil liberties rather than civil rights. Freedom of utterance and expression had, of course, been a long-time concern. Before the war he had often denounced the censors and the patrioteers. The flag wavers, he wrote in 1934, reminded him of vaudeville managers trying to save weak acts during the First World War: "A team of ham acrobats or a group of badly trained seals were coached to come into their finale brandishing the Stars and Stripes."[44] The function of political patriotism, he thought, was to disguise bad arguments, and he was merciless in exploring the implications, especially when he came to the Dies Committee in the late '30's.

He had lively memories of A. Mitchell Palmer and the

42 "The Easy Chair," *Harper's,* November 1944.
43 "The Easy Chair," *Harper's,* January 1946.
44 *Forays,* 159.

Red Scare of 1920, and he was alert for signs of a postwar reaction against individual freedom. When Homer Rainey was driven from the presidency of the University of Texas in 1945, DeVoto was quick to blow the whistle. "Here," he wrote, "is a naked form of the old terror: thinking is dangerous. Here are subversive, clear-minded men winning the support of honest, troubled men to another panic-stricken attack on education in the belief that education, which might be the interpreter and enlightened guide of change, is the begetter of change." This attack on academic freedom seemed to him "the first of a new model. As the waves of reaction gather strength in the years immediately ahead of the United States, the same attack will be made repeatedly, in many colleges, always by the same kind of men representing the same interests and forces, employing the same or equivalent means. What has happened to the University of Texas has happened to us all."[45]

The erosion of the Bill of Rights became almost his major theme in the late '40's. "The enemy is still the same," he wrote: "absolutism, authoritarianism, dictatorship, tyranny, whatever threatens freedom."[46] Long before Senator McCarthy first unfurled his fluctuating list of Communists in the State Department, DeVoto was in the forefront of the fight to defend privacy against the snoopers. His famous column "Due Notice to the FBI" was published four months before McCarthy made his speech at Wheeling. Here DeVoto sounded a splendid protest

[45] "The Dark Age in Texas," *Harper's*, August 1945.
[46] *Easy Chair*, 189.

against the spreading impression that "the interrogation of private citizens about other citizens is natural and justified." A single decade, he wrote, "has come close to making us a nation of common informers." All this, he said, has gone too far.

> We are dividing into the hunted and the hunters. There is loose in the United States today the same evil that once split Salem Village between the bewitched and the accused and stole men's reason quite away. We are informers to the secret police. Honest men are spying on their neighbors for patriotism's sake. We may be sure that for every honest man two dishonest ones are spying for personal advancement today and ten will be spying for pay next year.

DeVoto served public notice: he would no longer discuss any individual with any government representative. "I like a country," he wrote, "where it's nobody's damned business what magazines anyone reads, what he thinks, whom he has cocktails with . . . We had that kind of country only a little while ago and I'm for getting it back." When J. Edgar Hoover replied that he would not "dignify Mr. DeVoto's half-truths, inaccuracies, distortions, and misstatements with a denial or an explanation," DeVoto wondered whether an American citizen was not entitled to something better than this from the head of the Federal Bureau of Investigation. "Not dignifying," he said, "makes a neater game than answering criticism. It is also a form of loud-mouthed personal abuse, which has other names as well, by a man of great power and high public office."[47]

[47] *Easy Chair,* 175–76, 350.

The rise of McCarthy only stimulated DeVoto to further defiance. Nothing outraged him more in the early '50's than the respect accorded to the ex-Communist as an authority on loyalty and on history. "Before you can add a column of figures correctly," said DeVoto in a sardonic formulation of the McCarthy argument, "you must first add them wrong. He who would use his mind must first lose it. Various ex-communist intellectuals are offering themselves on just that basis as authorities about what has happened and guides to what must be done. Understand, I am right now *because* I . . . tried earlier to lead you astray. My intelligence has been vindicated *in that* it made an all-out commitment to error."[48]

No one, except DeVoto's friend Elmer Davis, wrote more effectively against what DeVoto called "the sickness of our time, the craziness of our time, the craziness in everyone."[49] Inevitably his defense of freedom guaranteed him the denunciation of McCarthy and his followers. In a nation-wide telecast in the 1952 campaign, indeed, McCarthy, to DeVoto's chagrin, angrily denounced him as "Richard" DeVoto. Little was more ironic than the attempt to portray DeVoto, who had been a scathing critic of the Communists twenty years before McCarthy had ever raised the issue, as a Communist sympathizer.

The fight for the Bill of Rights marked one great expression of DeVoto's postwar radical idealism. But perhaps an even more significant contribution — and one

[48] *Easy Chair*, 178.
[49] *Easy Chair*, 227.

which gave full expression to his love for the West and for
the land, the rivers, and the mountains of America — lay
in his battles in defense of the nation's resources. Even despite the war, the West had been at the center of DeVoto's
consciousness ever since his trip of 1940. The publication of *The Year of Decision: 1846* in 1943 was followed by *Across the Wide Missouri* in 1947, *The Course
of Empire* in 1952, and his edition of *The Journals of
Lewis and Clark* in 1953. Even his single novel of the
period was entitled *Mountain Time*. And his concern
with the West was as much contemporary as it was historical.

In 1946 he made an extended trip through the West.
He now began to see "the plundered province" in a deeper
perspective than he had in 1934; and, when he returned,
he set forth a new thesis — a thesis summarized in the title
of a piece for *Harper's*, "The West Against Itself." The
New Deal and the war, he felt, had given the West a new
opportunity for economic independence by laying the
basis for an industrial economy. The decision for the
West was whether it would seize this opportunity; and
what DeVoto now particularly noted was the role the
West was playing — and had always played — in its own
spoliation. The rich men of the West, he observed, were
in overwhelming majority allied with the system of ab-
sentee exploitation which had drained the West's resources
and wealth eastward. The West's "historic willingness to
hold itself cheap and its eagerness to sell out" were the
product of the West's own weaknesses. The West had

certainly been raped by the East, DeVoto said, but its posture had always invited rape. "Thus the basic problems are internal." If the East had not destroyed the resources of the West, the West would do so by itself. And his trip provided him new evidence of western schizophrenia. "There is intended," he wrote in *Harper's* in December 1946, "an assault on the public resources of the West which is altogether Western and so open that it cannot possibly be called a conspiracy. It is an assault which in a single generation could destroy the West and return it to the process of geology."[50]

With that passage, DeVoto signaled the beginning of a long and remarkable campaign to save the West from itself. He later said that the controversy over the public lands was the only one he ever deliberately precipitated.[51] The particular issue was an assault by the organized stockmen against the Forest Service and ultimately against the whole idea of a national domain. Cattlemen and sheepmen had long enjoyed the privilege of grazing their stock on certain public lands for the payment of a minimal fee and the observance of certain standards. The first objective of their new campaign was to transform this privilege into a vested right subject only to such regulation as they might impose on themselves. Beyond this, they planned a transfer of public lands in general from federal protection to the states. State governments, of course, could be coerced as the federal government could not be; and state owner-

50 "The Anxious West," *Harper's*, December 1946.
51 *Easy Chair*, 7.

ship would be a preliminary to turning the public lands over to private ownership at forced sale and at bargain prices (the price most commonly suggested was ten cents an acre). The Forest Service, in this stockmen's paradise, would be confined to rehabilitating land which lumbermen and stockmen had made unproductive under compulsion to transfer it to private ownership as soon as it had been made productive again. The ultimate goal was "to liquidate all public ownership of grazing land and forest land in the United States. And the wording of the resolution in which the U.S. Chamber of Commerce came to the support of the program *excepted no government land whatever.*"[52]

The stakes in the public lands could hardly be greater: an estimated 4 billion barrels of oil, enough oil shale to produce 130 billion barrels of crude oil, 111 trillion cubic feet of gas, 324 billion tons of coal, not to speak of timber, grass, electric power, water and minerals, the total value well over a trillion dollars — quite a lot to go on the cheap from the people to the oil companies, the timber companies, the mining companies, and the investment trusts. The result would be the biggest landgrab in American history and an incomparable steal by private interests. More than that, by removing these great tracts from federal control, this program would encourage overgrazing and other abuses of the land, damage the watersheds, lower the water table, and accelerate the whole terrible process of erosion.

[52] *Easy Chair*, 246–55.

At some point along the way, one is compelled to suppose, a steal of this proportion and with such catastrophic consequence would have been halted. That it was halted so rapidly and that the nation was spared so much needless destruction was the single-handed work of DeVoto. He was the first conservationist in nearly half a century (except Franklin D. Roosevelt) to command a national audience. His *Harper's* pieces alerted conservationists through the country, and the ensuing revolt of public opinion cut off the stockmen's legislative program of 1947 before it could get under way. In the 1948 election one senator (D'Ewart) and one congressman (Barrett of Wyoming) identified with the landgrab were retired to private life.

This was only the beginning of a fight which continued for the rest of DeVoto's days. He covered every sector of the battlefront with meticulous and passionate exactitude. Thrown back in one place, the stockmen counterattacked in another; and the change of administration in Washington in 1953 meant that, for the first time since Herbert Hoover had proposed that the unreserved public lands be turned over to the states, the stockmen and their associates had allies in the Executive Branch. DeVoto's last big piece on the subject, published in 1954, bore the somber title "Conservation: Down and on the Way Out." "In a year and a half," he wrote, "the businessmen in office have reversed the conservation policy by which the United States has been working for more than seventy years to substitute wise use of its natural resources in place of reckless destruction for the profit of special corporate interests.

They have reversed most of the policy, weakened all of it, opened the way to complete destruction. Every move in regard to conservation that the Administration has made has been against the public interest — which is to say against the future."[53] No man did more to rouse public opinion against this reversal than DeVoto. He was, in the phrase of his friend and ally Senator Richard Neuberger of Oregon, "the most illustrious conservationist who has lived in modern times."[54]

The conservation fight brought DeVoto into practical politics. During the '30's, his acquaintance with public officials and with politicians had been limited and accidental. But the future of the public lands was to be decided, of course, in the Congress; and in the course of his campaign DeVoto worked closely with senators and congressmen who shared his concern. Men like Lee Metcalf of Montana, Neuberger of Oregon, Paul Douglas of Illinois, Anderson of New Mexico became his friends. And he came to know well, too, many men in the government service. In 1949 Oscar Chapman, as Secretary of the Interior, appointed him a member of the National Parks Advisory Board. In the Forest Service itself, DeVoto had a score of staunch and faithful coworkers.

The culmination of his interest in politics came when Adlai Stevenson emerged as the leader of the Democratic party. The two men established a deep and lasting sympathy. Stevenson renewed DeVoto's faith in politics as a

---

[53] *Easy Chair*, 345.
[54] *New York Times,* September 25, 1960.

means of greatly serving the national welfare; DeVoto strengthened Stevenson's concern with the future of land and water and natural resources in America. DeVoto was far too good a writer to be useful as a draftsman of campaign speeches; but his spirit pervaded Stevenson's utterances on conservation in the 1952 campaign and even more in the years following. In 1954 the two men spent three or four days together in the Northwest inspecting the wilderness and contemplating the national ruin which lay ahead if the give-away programs should ever succeed.

The fight for conservation, the fight for civil freedom, the fight for Adlai Stevenson — in this succession of battles DeVoto's radical idealism came to its fine maturity. He never became the kind of *a priori* liberal he had detested in the '30's; his skepticism, the hard, rough edge of his mind, persisted to the end. But in these last years he applied his skepticism unsparingly to the pretensions of power and in so doing helped keep open essential options for his fellow countrymen. His broader view of democracy remained tempered and sardonic. This was perhaps the fundamental reason for his closeness to Adlai Stevenson — an intimacy he would not have achieved, or perhaps cared to achieve, with less reflective and complex political leaders, even those he came to admire, like Franklin Roosevelt and Wendell Willkie.

He had given his own sense of democracy poignant expression twenty years before his death. He was speaking at the University of Missouri on the writer who lay closest to his heart and in whose work he had been immersed so much of his life — Mark Twain. "In our day,"

DeVoto mused, "has perished the New Jerusalem of the democratic hope." Democracy, once so ecstatic in its visions, had begun to recognize the limits of the human predicament. "It was learning to come to terms not only with realities but with self-knowledge. Neither man nor society, it was coming slowly to perceive, had in itself the seeds of perfection." Mark Twain had been among the first to understand these things — to understand that democracy could rise no higher than its source and that its source was the human race, for which old Mark, as DeVoto noted, was willing to find the conclusive adjective.

"He had been called a pessimist," DeVoto wrote of Mark Twain. "Pessimism is only the name that men of weak nerves give to wisdom. Say rather that, when he looked at the human race, he saw no ranked battalions of the angels . . . Say that with a desire however warm and with the tenderness of a lover, he nevertheless understood that the heart of man is wayward, a dark forest. Say that it is not repudiation he comes to at last, but reconciliation — an assertion that democracy is not a pathway to the stars but only the articles of war under which the race fights an endless battle with itself.[56]

This was, as DeVoto saw it, the meaning of democracy. And fighting such a battle, DeVoto might have added, vindicates democracy by producing men of compassion, of courage and of faith. Such men justify the battle and renew the strength and decency of a civilization. Bernard DeVoto was such a man. We all stand profoundly in his debt.

[56] *Forays,* 370–71.

The Personality

by
Wallace Stegner

I F I HAD any temptation to turn this memoir into a testimonial, the memory of Benny DeVoto's round, brown,
goggled, sardonic eye would be enough to strike the impulse dead. Being from Utah, he knew about testimonial
meetings. It is better simply to record a little about him
and try to understand him; praise and blame came to roost
in Benny's loft so constantly that from his earliest youth
he must have heard them quarreling at his eaves. He
earned the one and risked the other, and I do not need to
add to either. And if I address myself somewhat personally to the pleasure of talking about him, I do not apolo-
gize, for though in November 1960 he is five years dead,
he is still personal to me.

Begin at the beginning of my knowledge of him. One
morning in 1925, when I was a freshman at the University of Utah, I came into the English building just as a
professor yanked open his office door and hurled a magazine into the hall. The offensive journal was *The American Mercury*, about which even I, and even in Salt Lake

City, had heard, and the obviously offending part of it was an article entitled "Utah," by Bernard DeVoto. It was a calculated piece of mayhem that out-Menckened Mencken. Though I have not looked at it for thirty-five years, I have a vivid recollection that it said dreadful things about the state where I lived. Apparently we were the ultimate, final, and definitive home of the Boob. We were owned by Boston banks and the Copper Trust, and bamboozled by the Church of Jesus Christ of Latter-day Saints, an institution whose beliefs would bring a baboon to incredulous laughter but whose business acuteness had made it a director of a hundred corporations. This Utah occupied the fairest mountains and valleys on the footstool and grew the best peaches ever grown and had a history of dedication and heroism, in however dubious a cause. But it lived now, as in its founding years, by fantasy, myth, and wishful thinking, and it demonstrated all too faithfully the frontier curve from piety through property to vulgarity. It was conventional, stuffy, provincial, hypocritical, deluded; it had never produced a writer, sculptor, painter, statesman, soldier, scholar, or distinguished man of any sort, it was terrified of any expression of mind, there were not fifteen people in the whole state for whom signing their own names was not an effort.

And so on, a considerable mouthful, spit out with a vigor and venom that only the twenties or Bernard DeVoto, or the two in combination, could have generated. I did not then know anything about the Village Virus or any of the robust literary antibiotics that were being used against it; nor did I know any of the personal reasons that made Mr. DeVoto so angry at Utah and especially his home city of Ogden. I simply let myself be swept up in the happy vehemence of his rhetoric, though even then I suppose I must have understood that a lot of what he said was exaggerated and unjust. If he got a few innocent bystanders, I was willing to sacrifice them for the pleasure of looking upon the more deserving corpses.

As an introduction to DeVoto, that article could have been improved upon, and DeVoto himself never thought enough of it to include it in any of his collections of essays. Nevertheless it expressed him. It had his chosen and almost compulsive subject, the West. It had his habit of challenge and overstatement set off from a launching pad of fact. It had his frequent mixture of the lyrical (when dealing with scenery, say, or peaches, or the beauty of Utah girls) and the vituperative (when dealing with most aspects of society, education, institutions, interests, delusions, or public characters). It had also his incomparable knack of infuriating people. But learn one trick, which most of his readers and all of his friends learned quickly enough: learn to discount him ten to twenty percent for showmanship, indignation, and the inevitable warping power of his gift for language, and there remained one of the sanest, most acute, most rooted-in-the-ground observers of American life that we have had. He wrote dozens of essays out of indignation or with short-term objectives; these he seldom collected, but let them die. The ones that were close to his considered convictions he kept, and often revised. When he caught himself in exaggeration or error, as he did when he came to collect some of his early essays on education, he cheerfully ate crow. For despite a reputation as a wild man or an ogre, he was open always to the persuasion of facts. He seldom dealt in the outrageous merely for the sake of outraging, though he knew the dramatizing value of shock, and used it. His exaggerations were likely to be extensions of observed truth; and when he was wrong, as he surely sometimes was, he was wrong in the right directions. If he said, in effect, that American civilization was sleeping with every bum in town, there was almost certainly *someone* in her bed.

He had a gift for indignation — which means only that he believed some things passionately and could not contain himself when he saw them endangered by knaves or fools; and however ironic and detached he tried to be, he could become a Galahad in a cause that enlisted as much of him as did the conservation and public lands fights of the late 1940's and 1950's. He began and remained an unfriendly critic of Mormonism, but his half-Mormon heritage and background had bred a good deal of Mormon moralizing into him. Even his peculiar brand of eloquence, at once biblical, orotund, and salty, is related to the eloquence of some celebrated Mormon preachers such as J. Golden Kimball. Like Kimball, Benny could thunder colloquially. Once at Bread Loaf, Vermont, I heard him deliver a sort of lay sermon — let us say it was on the necessity of acknowledging what is under our noses, one of his recurrent themes — and in the course of his talk he got so worked up he brought on a terrible electrical storm that knocked the lights out. No one was in the least surprised; it seemed the most natural thing in the world, the anticipable consequence of the pulpit oratory that went on thundering out of the dark.

But that was much later, a full quarter century after that angry boy, talented and educated beyond his native environment, had fled Ogden with the manuscript of his first novel under his arm. When he wrote his diatribe against Utah, and by extension the whole Rocky Mountain West, he was a young instructor at Northwestern, the author of two novels, beginning to be known as a writer for the magazines, an angry young man full of the heady rebellions of the twenties, with talents that he knew were notable, and with fears of himself that sucked him down into spells of despair and darkness. He was as hot with aspiration as a turpentined mule, an ardent, extravagant, romantic, idealistic, indignant young man with a future. And despite his fears about himself and his fits of depression, he had some notion what that future would involve.

Among the DeVoto Papers at Stanford University is a letter to Melville Smith dated October 22, 1920. In it young DeVoto's natural ebullience is compounded by the fact that when he wrote it he was recovering from a disappointment in love and from a perhaps consequent nervous illness. Nevertheless it may be taken seriously. It was Benny's lifetime habit to bounce high when he was thrown hard, and to fall farther the higher he bounced. "I burst," he said:

> I burst with creative criticism of America — I have at last found a kind of national self-consciousness. Not the mighty   anvil-on-which-is-hammered-out-the-future-of-the-world. Still less the damned-bastard-parvenu-among-the-nations. But I have begun to see American history with some unity, with some perspective, with some meaning . . . to dare to think from cause to effect, from the past to the present and future, always with this curious new sense of yea-saying youth.
>
> I do not commit the historic folly, from Washington Irving to Van Wyck Brooks, of hearing fiddles tuning up all over America . . . But I have dared at last to believe that the Nation begins to emerge from adolescence into young manhood, that hereafter the colossal strength may begin to count for the better, as well as for the worse. That indeed we have come to say yea, at last.
>
> And in the facts which alone can show whether we take the turn, or in the study of them, I shall, I think, spend my vigorous years . . . I believe I have found something into which I may pour that arresting, God-awful emulsion that is I.

Even the friendliest reader will find both self-dramatizing and turgidity in that manifesto, and Benny is surely a figure of the twenties as he says yea to America with one side of his mouth while saying nay to Ogden, the Village, with the other. The earnestness, however, is real, the dedication is real, the repudiation of certain effusive ideas is real (even a favorite whipping boy is anticipated), and the impulse toward history, toward the study of cause and effect in the making of American civilization, is sig-

nificant. Young Milton impatiently strengthening his
wings for broader flights, hypnotized by the novel that
was the mirror of his emotional turmoil (its title was
"Cock Crow," and the manuscript is among his papers at
Stanford), he countered emotional strain by dreaming of
an effort more stringently intellectual than fiction. Con-
stitutionally a believer and a yea-sayer, but already suspicious of literary criticism and other forms of "beautiful
thinking," he had even at twenty-three a faith in knowledge, in facts; but there were some facts that he did not yet
know, one of them being that it was the West, which he
scorned, that he most wanted to say yea to. During the
next thirty-five years, the "vigorous years" of his dedication, he would be many things — novelist, professor,
editor, historian, pamphleteer, critic, and under a half
dozen aliases, hack writer — with such range and in such
profusion that no neat classification can hold him. Visible
in his God-awful emulsion along with the scissors and snails
and puppy dogs' tails, as real an ingredient as the irritable
idealism and the scorn and the skinless self-doubt, would
be a belligerent professionalism. He would pride himself
on being a pro, would wear the discipline of deadlines and
editorial specifications like a hair shirt, because he despised
literary phonies, narcissistic artists, public confessors,
gushers, long-hairs, and writers of deathless prose; and he
would despise these because he feared them in himself.
All through Benny's life, a submerged romantic, a literary
Harvard boy from Copey's class, would send up embarrassing bubbles of gas, and one way to cover these mo-

ments would be the overt belch of professionalism. Professionalism would lead him, too, to take on many kinds of literary jobs — articles, introductions, magazine stories and serials, political speech-writing, reviews — and he would work himself punishingly. In self-defense he would affect to mistrust the imagination and value the hard head, hard work, hard facts; but certain things would not change, he would retain his contradictions.

His repudiation of his western birthright would not stick; the West would not let him go so casually. He would have to come back and worry its complacent provincials and its Two-Gun Desmonds, deflate its myths, expose its economics and its politics, and tell its story in half a hundred essays, half a dozen novels, several works of criticism, and a monumental series of histories. Debunking or correcting western myths, scorning the things the West had become, he would continue to love, to the point of passion, western openness, freedom, air, scenery, violence; and would accept some of the myths as eagerly as the most illiterate cowhand reading *Western Stories* in the shade of the cookhouse. In all his literary jobs he would be a wholly competent workman; in some, as in his hymn to alcohol called *The Hour*, he would be delightful; in many, as in his pamphleteering essays, he would be splendid. But when he wrote history, when he brought together the whole story of the West as frontier, as dream and discovery, exploration and confrontation, he would be magnificent.

The variety of DeVoto's literary work reflects intellectual and physical vitality, not a groping. Though he did many things on the side, he found his field early, worked at it steadily, and brought it to a triumphant bumper crop in his trilogy of histories. But in thus fulfilling the somewhat incoherent program he had set for himself in 1920, he did not quite comprehend all America as cause and effect, promise and payoff. Not even his appetite for work could accomplish so much — and nostalgia, moreover, is a local emotion. Nostalgia, the release of dammed images, memories, feelings, would be necessary for his imaginative re-creation of the frontier. Whenever Benny's mind and emotions could be brought into phase, when Cambridge could bridge time and space back to Weber Canyon, he wrote as he was manifestly born to write, and produced what a continued residence in the West would have made difficult, but what exile made inevitable.

Without committing the error of imagining an Ordeal of Benny DeVoto, one must insist on the importance of alienation and exile. He was born on a frontier as the frontier was passing, when there was no future for frontiersmen, and division and doubt were in him from birth, for his mother was the daughter of a pioneer Mormon farmer (see "The Life of Jonathan Dyer") and his father, the son of an Italian cavalry officer, was an intellectual, a Catholic, "a man of great brilliance and completely paralyzed will," a total outsider. To go to a Catholic school in a Mormon community, to be the only boy in a roomful of girls, to be brilliant and bookish where brilliance and bookishness had (he came to think) neither audience nor function nor reward — these were only aggravations of a dislocation already begun. Of the seven children of his grandfather, not one stayed on the farm or in the Mormon Church; of all the children and grandchildren, "only the novelist, a romantic," ever revisited the home place after the death of the man who had grubbed it out of the sagebrush and irrigated it into fertility.

A divided inheritance can give a boy parallax, he has a base for triangulation and judgment, but he will never be quite at home in his home. And brilliance, especially when associated with insecurity and assertiveness, can isolate a child as effectively as if the disapproving community had shut him in the closet of his mind. It was in his mind that he lived, there and in the canyons of the Wasatch that let him play at independence, freedom, and self-reliance. The limitations and frustrations of Ogden could be transcended on lonely expeditions, by the practice of partly imaginary survival skills, by feats that tested him where there was no chance of being seen and humiliated, by the comfort of wilderness, by the whistle of marmots in mountain meadows, by the eternal sound of mountain water always passing and always there. The most lyrical of his 1920 letters to Melville Smith describes just such a healing expedition. Many years later, in Cambridge, I used sometimes to get desperate telephone calls from Benny: "Come on and walk me around Fresh Pond!" And when we were spending summers in Vermont there would come letters: "Is there anywhere on your place where a man can walk

— walk a long way, off the roads, in the woods? Is there any place where a man can shoot a .22?"

It is entirely possible that like many lonely children young Bernard DeVoto didn't recognize his trouble as loneliness, but I am sure it was. That shooting, for instance. Shooting was his favorite boyhood sport — and there is no lonelier sport unless it is rowing. But where rowing is mindless, subduing body and mind to a rhythm, lulling identity to sleep, shooting is another thing. Marksmanship can not only fill empty time, it can feed fantasy, for you can put any face you want on the black dot of the bullseye, and the process of shooting holes in it is not only skill, which is comforting, but revenge, which is sweet.

Because I grew up on a frontier even cruder than Weber Canyon, and was halved and quartered away from wholeness at least as early as Benny DeVoto, I think I can imagine him as a boy. Probably he was a little brattish, he showed off before girls, teachers, and God; he was contentious, captious, critical, quick to scorn; he affected superiorities and was constantly in controversies and in his bad spells was desolated that some people didn't like him. He was devoted to certain people, ideas, books, with a fanatical devotion, an ardent, unreasonable extremity. He got crushes on girls and for a week or a month was in a frenzy to immolate himself, and within another week or month had discovered that the blonde goddess was dim-witted. Nevertheless his real friendships were affectionate, lasting, and utterly loyal — there have been few people to whom friendship meant more. He read furiously, always beyond his years, and if he used his reading to impress people, that would not be strange. The fact is, he couldn't *not* read. His brain was as busy as a woodpecker, it pecked at him all day and at night perched ominously just above the lintel of sleep, as disturbing as Poe's raven. Probably even at ten or twelve he had migraines — certainly he had them later. He was a problem to his parents and a terror to the conventional and a despair to his teachers, and he learned early, being an outsider, and different, to fling the acid of his scorn into the face of provincial Ogden, already too small a world for him.

He tried the University of Utah for a year, and that too, in 1914–1915, was such a small world that he stirred it like a porpoise in a Paddock Pool. After one year he was off to Harvard, and now he found himself for the first time in a world profoundly, self-consciously, intellectual. If he did not quite grapple with Greek and Hebrew verbs all day and then take a walk in Mount Auburn Cemetery for recreation, he did the equivalent. He devoured books. He was inspired by great teachers, including Copey, and he met people of his own age whom he could not cow: boys as bright as he, better read, better disciplined, boys who tamed some of his exuberances and shamed him out of some of his provincial prejudices, but who at the same time — and this would be sweet — found him something new and special, amusing or arresting, a wild man from the West, a sensitive intellectual out of the howling wilderness of Utah. He never quite got over the role — and the role, observe, was a double one.

At Harvard he crossed a sort of intellectual South Pass the way it was first crossed in fact — eastward — and saw something of what opened up beyond. On the dubious side, he was corroborated in his literary and idealistic posturing: ("Thank God for Harvard. It has given me a thorough-going contempt for these externals. Harvard took me and turned me inward, showed me the heart of things, set burning a lamp in the sanctuary of the ideal. Harvard has shown me that the flesh is nothing beside the spirit . . ."). But he learned too that his native West was interesting, even romantic, to Cambridge eyes and to the eyes of nostalgia, and that it was a splendid place for illustrating pure aspiration dragged down by philistinism. He began to play aficionado about his country, as a hundred thousand western boys have played it in eastern colleges. Being Benny DeVoto, he would have taken the trouble to back up his brags or his diatribes with reading; somewhere very early he began to read western history, geography, exploration, travel, and he read them avidly all his life. (Once he told me cynically that as a journalist he had learned to make a fact go a long way, which was true. It was also true that few people ever collect as many facts about their specialty as he collected about the West. He was loaded, a learned man, and he had the ease with his information that great familiarity brings. In Robert Frost's phrase, he could swing what he knew.)

At Harvard too (I am guessing, but I would back my guess with a bet) he was confirmed in a habit that regional folklore and personal insecurity had already formed in

him: the belief or pretense that true vigor, including intellectual vigor, is always a little bit crude and aggressive.
During the course of his career he offended some people
with the consequences of that assumption, which remained
part of his critical method. He scared a lot of others with
his cartwheeling and shooting, and some of them never
did comprehend that often he was only riding up in his
warpaint to shake hands.

Finally Harvard must have encouraged him, in his role
of western wild man, to hunt the picturesque and sul-
phurous phrasing of a man who split a plank every time
he spit. Impolite western literature furnished him excel-
lent models, including Mark Twain; there have been few
if any moderns who could handle spreadeagle invective
as Benny could.

Whatever poses he adopted or roles he assumed, the
self-doubting youth was still there, and would remain
there. Among the DeVoto Papers is a series of letters
written to his parents when he was in OCS camp at Camp
Lee, Virginia, in 1918. Even to one who knew and loved
Benny well, they are a revelation. As a son, however
much unrest he might have given his parents (and he was
fond of remarking later that the only torture worse than
being a parent was being a child), he was an agonizedly affectionate son. In those letters he throbs and yearns and
aspires in a way that begins by being almost embarrassing
and ends by being touching. If there was ever a boy who
needed love, faith, praise, reassurance, and who hoped to
deserve them, hoped humbly to earn them, it was he. The

need for the safety and reassurance of friends, too, persisted throughout his life. His letters were often intensely personal, a pouring out of aspiration, confession, self-analysis, self-blame, a release of gas from the submerged affection-craving boy, freed in the privacy of love or friendship from the necessity of deceptive belches and hoots and catcalls.

One of the tenderest things I know about Benny — one of the tenderest things I ever heard about anybody — is unfortunately sequestered in the Stanford Library vaults for a good many years because of the personal nature of some of its references. This is the correspondence between Benny and Kate Sterne, a shut-in tubercular patient who had written him a fan letter to which Benny, as he always did, courteously replied. She wrote again, he replied again, and before long he was periodically relaxing after a hard day's work by writing her long eruptive midnight letters. He took down his hair and said what he thought about those who had offended or slighted or pleased him, he wept for lost battles and exulted for victories, he analyzed people and events and policies and regions, assessed reputations, let air out of balloons. The correspondence continued from 1933 until 1944, when Kate Sterne died. Some day it will make a touching and wonderful book, because the invalid became for Benny the most intimate confidante, and his letters constitute a secret, indiscreet, uninhibited diary of eleven of his most active years. What is more to the point here, they kept Kate Sterne alive and mentally engaged long after she might have been expected to be dead. He dedicated *The Year of Decision, 1846* to her, he told her things that he would never have put in print and that he perhaps never told another living soul. And he never met her, not so much as to shake hands.

To young Bernard DeVoto, wild intellectual from the Rocky Mountains, rebel, iconoclast, and idealist, the war came like a tornado that uproots trees and houses. He enlisted in a tumult of patriotism. It is hard to remember and believe the faith that young men once had that they might save the world for democracy. Benny had that faith, had it like *paralysis agitans*. Quite seriously, he was ready to die with an inspiring phrase on his lips. Accentuating the spirit, he immediately began a novel, writing it in his head because boot camp gave him no time for pen and paper, "a novel of my own country, the wide and ample theatre of the hills, the peaks and valleys, the mountain streams, the railroads, above all the people . . . If ever there was a labor of love it is the construction of this book, into which I am putting all the knowledge that has come to me . . . Already I have written much of a unique book, of a book which touches depths of feeling I had not know[n], which is the expression of my most outstretched aspiration . . ."

It does not sound like the DeVoto we know. And yet this was the tender thing that never quit living in Benny's shell. From Camp Lee he wrote asking his family to preserve his letters for their possible historical value, and he corresponded thereafter with posterity's perhaps-critical eye on him: "What kind of a man do these missives show

me to be? Is there any hope, do you think, for my ultimate salvation?" He took pride in bearing up under heat
and fatigue, and we see suddenly that in Ogden this wild
man was probably thought a sissy: "I am no weakling after
all, despite the sneers I have known in the past." As the
camp progressed and he found he could measure himself
against the others without apology, he grew cocky, and
out of one letter scrawled in a tent in the breathless
Virginia heat bursts a salvo of pure DeVoto, in color and
tone, exuberance and hyperbole, a foretaste of the bump-
tiousness of his maturity:

What need shall I have of a wife? I have learned to cook
my meals and wash my dishes, to make my bed and sweep
the floor, to clean, wash, and mend my clothes, to arrange
all my belongings and possessions with a neatness and accu-
racy unknown to women. Why should I ever call a doctor?
I know how to keep myself trim and healthy, know the infallibility of iodine and C.C. pills — the Army's own medi-
cines — and know all the approved methods of treating every
injury from dysentery to disembowellment, from sunstroke
to a cracked knuckle. Practical rubbing up against all kinds
of men, the lectures of many officers, and the clean thoughts
of a healthy body have taught me more ethics and morality
than any minister possibly could. I am or am becoming as-
tronomer and surveyor, indian scout and clerk, statistician
and prospector, woodsman, artist, farmer — every trade and
employment within the seven seas. I dare go alone into the
wilderness confident that, within a week, I could build me a
forty room villa with lawns, garden and garage: fit it out
with furniture; grow, kill, and cook my own food; set up a
religion and code of laws; establish industry and train an
army; organize departments of public health and finance —

and, in short, build me a State with no other tools than an
intrenching spade and a cartridge belt.

Posterity might wink, but the cockiness, like some other
DeVoto exaggerations, was built on facts. He graduated
7th — apologizing to his parents for not doing better — in
a class of 150. But he did not get overseas; he was too
good a rifle shot, he had improved the loneliness of Ogden
to too good purpose, and he wound up in Camp Perry,
Ohio, as a musketry instructor.

He did not know it, but that was as close as he would
ever get to going abroad. He would make certain Pro-
hibition-years excursions into Canada in search of the rye
and bourbon that he called the two greatest American
inventions ("How is it that every time I go to Canada the
word gets around the neighborhood by osmosis and I have
a hundred solicitous friends?") and in the later years of
World War II he would suffer himself to be inoculated
against typhoid, tetanus, yellow fever, and other plagues,
preparatory to going to Africa to write the history of the
African campaigns for the War Department. But something happened to that. He did not go, and he never got
off the continent of North America. It was just as well.
On that continent he could be an expert and a specialist.

After the Armistice Lieutenant DeVoto went back to
Harvard to finish, and was told by a member of the faculty
not to take himself too seriously, and resolved to follow
that advice. After that he returned to Ogden to write his
first novel ("a disgustingly immature production for one
who asserts so much maturity as I"), to fall in love and be

jilted ("The fiction of romantic love is not likely again to impose on me"), to address the University Club on American liberty and get himself expelled, to conduct with vigor his war against all that Ogden stood for ("Do not forget that at best I am a spore in Utah, not adapted to the environment, a maverick who may not run with the herd, unbranded, given an ill name. These people are not my people, their God is not mine . . ."), to suffer a nervous collapse ("I have a peculiar capacity for suffering in those areas of personality which neither anatomy nor psychology has yet been able to describe — areas inextricably tangled with religion and sex and faith and poetry"), and in general to take himself very seriously indeed. He was emancipated by an offer to teach English at Northwestern, and so fled the Babylonian captivity of his native city. He found places where his mind could work effectively, if not in peace — Evanston, New York, especially Cambridge — and settled into furious pursuit of the distinction that he yearned for. From there on, it is the career we know.

The weight and effect of a maverick's career is not immediately assessable, and in DeVoto's case the assessment, when it comes, will have to be a composite one, for no single biographer or critic is likely to be able to follow him into all the corners of American life where he had authority or exerted influence. Nevertheless the outlines of his lasting reputation seem already reasonably clear. At least it may be worth while to indicate one's personal preferences, to state what seems most important as one looks back over the work of a man who remains so stubbornly alive. When he died, one's first thought after the shock of loss was "Who will do his work? Who can carry on what he did?" For it was never so apparent as when death stopped it that for many years he had done at least three men's work, and that it would take three very good men indeed to replace him — that in fact there was not an adequate replacement for any fraction of him.

As a novelist he does not seem truly important, though it was novelist he set out to be. He used to tell students that until a man had written five novels he had no right to call himself a novelist, by which he meant a pro. By that definition Benny qualified, for under his own name he published six and wrote a seventh and part of an eighth, and under the pseudonym of John August he wrote four others. He made a clear distinction between his serious novels and those he wrote as serial entertainments for the magazines — not that he wanted to play demi-virgin, but that his magazine serials were frankly written for money and he did not value them. His serious novels he did value; the inscriptions to his father in copies of his first three books indicate awareness that performance has not quite lived up to desire, but they insist that these are honest books, as true to fact as he can make them, as good as he can do. They also reflect his preoccupation with the West, for *The Crooked Mile* and *The House of Sun-Goes-Down* chronicle the development of a western town not unlike Ogden, *The Chariot of Fire* is the story of a frontier prophet and martyr not unlike Joseph Smith, and even the last one, *Mountain Time*, which begins in a New York hospital, brings its hero Cy Kinsman back to his western birthplace for a sort of reconciliation of the exile that Benny himself had gone through.

These are all honest books and competent ones, and except for *The Crooked Mile*, which sprawls rather badly toward the end, they are well-carpentered, witty, packed with observation and ideas. But for me at least the thrill of life is not in them. The eloquence sounds a little wrong when put in the mouths of fictional characters, the dialogue often glitters but seldom falls exactly right on the ear. There is some dreams-of-glory posturing, especially in the early ones: Benny's heroes have a facility for attracting gorgeous women and for knocking down stupids, sots, and other denizens of the modern West. *Mountain Time*, which seems to me the best of the five novels, contains a detailed and persuasive look at the medical profession, besides characters who move and talk with a great deal more naturalness. But Cy Kinsman in that novel tends to repeat Gordon Abbey of *The Crooked Mile,* and the paralysis of the will that marks them both seems more a contrivance to delay a denouement than something the characters couldn't help.

In short, the fault in these novels seems to me to be that they lean too hard on contrivance, they never quite become life, they are tainted — *et ego peccavi,* Benny! — with the literary, a thing that Benny himself despised. The romantic idealist of the youthful letters, the literary young man from Copey's class, shows through more

clearly in the novels than in any of the other writings, and
it is an inescapable fact that DeVoto is less sure in his
handling of emotional situations in the novels than he is,
say, in the reporting of Mark Twain's *Wanderjahre*, of
the hardships of the Mormon migration, or the ecology of
fur hunters. *Mark Twain's America*, which came between
his third and fourth novels, showed him for the first time
at something like his full powers. He must himself have
recognized that he wrote much better, more authoritatively, more pungently, more importantly, when he could
not only write out of the western experience that he
knew best, but when he could speak in his own tone of
voice, without the ventriloquisms of fiction. Then information, lyricism, irony, indignation, the habit of hyperbole and picturesque phrase-making, could all come together, and Benny's emotional attitudes, though they are
evident, are evident at some distance; they inform the facts
but are not dwelt on; they produce something very like
the tone and inflection of a voice, the stop and flow and
rise and fall and thunder and hush of a knowing, intelligent, committed, and unremittingly interested observer.

   DeVoto's first significant notice came not because of his
novels but because of his essays in *American Mercury*,
Harper's, and other magazines. They are the beginning
of his lifelong career in social criticism and pamphleteering; the essay on Utah that I read in 1925 was one of
them, and it, like dozens of others, was never collected and
is not likely to be. Typical is what happened to a whole
series of angry essays on education written during the

five years at Northwestern. Reviewing them in 1936 for possible inclusion in *Forays and Rebuttals*, Benny found most of them "outrageously over-simplified" and others, such as the much anthologized "The Co-Eds: God Bless Them," to be "in some part untrue, in greater part obvious and irrelevant, and in no part profound." Less than a third of his essay production up to that time seemed to him worth reprinting, and his judgment was probably right. But even with a casualty rate of 66 per cent, DeVoto's essays in social criticism, including the magnificent series on western land problems and conservation reprinted in *The Easy Chair* just before his death, retain an astonishing vitality. I doubt that any body of like essays from the twenties, thirties, and forties would prove, on examination, to have dated so little, and some of them in their time were of robust usefulness in causes that I cannot but think good.

Who spoke any more forthrightly or effectively against irresponsible Congressional red-hunting than Benny did in "Guilt by Distinction," a mordant undressing of the Reece Committee? Who among us did not cheer when in "Due Notice to the FBI" Benny spoke our minds? ("Representatives of the FBI and of other official investigating bodies have questioned me, in the past, about a number of people and I have answered their questions. That's over. . . . If it is my duty as a citizen to tell what I know about someone, I will perform that duty under subpoena, in open court, before that person and his attorney . . .") Whether he was fighting the battle of freedom or protesting the pasteurization of cheese, exposing the land-grab plans of western stock interests or bringing to bear lessons of history upon the problems of the present, DeVoto as essayist performed public services greater than those of most public servants, and during his twenty years in the "Easy Chair" he built up not only an effective information organization but an enormous and respectful countrywide audience. When students of the future come to sift the scores of essays that he threw off at white heat all his life, a good many are going to be found to be not only reprintable but as near as such things come to being permanent, a part of the tradition, a part of the literature. "I stand on the facts," Benny said about his rejected education articles. "I should not care to stand on all the conclusions." Of a couple of fat booksful of his total production he could stand on the conclusions as well, and on some of them he would not even have to grant the customary discount.

The essayist who began as an amusing wild man grew into one of the most respected voices of the public conscience. His parallel and interwoven career as a literary critic does not show the same upward and rising curve. He fell away from literary criticism, in fact, as he fell away from fiction, because at bottom he was suspicious of it. His first successful book, *Mark Twain's America*, he called neither history nor biography nor literary criticism, though it was in some part all three, but an "essay in the correction of ideas." In that book his mind was speaking not only against a critical and psychological theory and not only against Van Wyck Brooks, but against a whole habit of mind and — never forget it — against the irresponsible literary romantic in his own house. An anti-literary bias, a sometimes belligerent philistinism, marked much of his criticism and marred some of it. Whether he was attacking Malcolm Cowley, in a review of *Exile's Return*, for assuming that the expatriates constituted a whole American writing generation, or whether he was tempestuously rejecting Thomas Wolfe's undiscipline in "Genius is Not Enough," he hammered at the need for knowledge, information, facts, and on top of those, professional discipline. Never having been abroad, he looked with skepticism upon the exiles; too often feeling truly lost, he did not want to be part of any lost generation. And anyway, his exile did not reach so far. He had found in New England an intellectual climate that he liked and in which he could work; and in the American scene, past and present, he had found adequate subject matter. Not to find these things seemed to him a literary affectation; and he knew something about literary poses, for he had been there.

So the best of Benny's criticism is related to the most American of all our writers, Mark Twain, of whose papers he was curator from 1938 to 1946. Already addicted to the disciplines of history, he based *Mark Twain's America*, as he said, solidly on the works themselves, as he based *Mark Twain in Eruption* and *Mark Twain at Work* solidly on the manuscript papers. Even in his examination of the despairing backgrounds of *The Mysterious Stranger*, one of the most speculative of his literary studies, he built his speculation on a foundation of manuscripts, false starts, scraps, letters; and when he started what other scholars have turned into a continuing search for the key to the composition of *Huckleberry Finn* he proceeded from evidence, not from a theory.

All his life, that is, he had a quarrel with the habit of making literary judgments about life, what he finally came to call the "literary fallacy." The little book by that title, first given as a series of lectures at the University of Indiana, was the summation of ideas implicit or explicit in all his criticism from *Mark Twain's America* on, and it more or less marked DeVoto's retirement from literary criticism. It is a book which must be taken at the customary discount, and it precipitated a painful literary quarrel. Also, in some eyes it marked Benny as a philistine. If being a philistine means valuing facts and suspecting attitudinizers, he was; a belligerent one of a kind it is healthy to have around. Presented with dream boats, he was likely to make pragmatic tests such as stepping on the starter to see if the motor ran.

Philistine or not, he was a healthy and skeptical influence in a profession likely to be full of hot air; Mark Twain criticism could use him right now. Though he was perhaps somewhat less important as a literary critic than as a gadfly of the public conscience, he was still a critic of range, depth, vigor, and a consistent point of view, and in the area which he made his specialty he was major. But in neither social criticism nor literary criticism was he so important as in history. There he brought off something monumental, massive, grandly conceived and beautifully controlled, a three-volume history of the West as imagination and reality and realization. *The Course of Empire, Across the Wide Missouri,* and *The Year of Decision, 1846* seem to me to warrant all the superlatives that they have consistently won; they belong on the shelf that contains only Prescott, Bancroft, Motley, Adams, and Parkman, and they are not unworthy of the company they find there. In every way they were the climax of Benny DeVoto's career, and with them he won the absolute distinction that he aspired to. The novels seem, in view of this achievement, like experiments in the tricks of dramatizing action and revealing character; the literary criticism like a course in the estimating of documents; the historical essays like finger exercises; the edition of Lewis and Clark's *Journals* like an encore. The real program of this career was the trilogy of histories.

They are, for one thing, incredibly learned. Their pages are a web of cross-reference and allusion, packed with facts, crowded with brilliant historical portraits. A lifetime of reading and study is distilled in them, and the mistrust with which Benny regarded his romantic and literary lesser half led him to work by preference from original documents, to the sharp intensification of dramatic effect. There is, moreover, more than mere information; these are not merely history as record, they are history as literature. And here the frontier boyhood and the personal acquaintance with country and weather, landscape and coloring and quality of light, drouth and distance, paid off. These histories are related to Parkman's in their quality of personal participation, in the way history can be felt on the skin and in the muscles because the author himself has been able to imagine it that way, having taken the trouble to live as much of it as possible himself.

This way, at least, the exile who never fully admitted he was an exile came home. This is a better and fuller reconciliation than he arranged for his character Cy Kinsman, who rather unrealistically wound up teaching physiology in a cow college. Reconciliation might have proceeded even farther if Benny had lived a little longer, for when he died he was working on the manuscript of a book to be called *The Western Paradox*. Except for one "Easy Chair" on literary cowboys, it had got no farther than a rough draft, and Mrs. DeVoto decided, wisely I think, not to let it be published. Reconciliation or not, the full fusion of western past and western present, of the local realities and the exiled intelligence, it would have been anticlimactic unless he had been able to take it through the second and third drafts that put the sting into his prose and the bite into his ideas. And even without it, he had done enough. More than enough.

A Bibliography of the Writings of Bernard DeVoto

by
Julius P. Barclay

WITH THE COLLABORATION
OF ELAINE HELMER PARNIE

Preface

In *Minority Report* DeVoto outlined the pitfalls for his bibliographers:

> I am a professional writer, a journalist, and am proud of the craft. . . . As a journalist I have ranged pretty widely. I am an educated man and am willing to write about anything I am informed about and interested in. On occasions when we have drunk beer together Mr. Elmer Davis (he and Robert Frost are the literary people with whom I least need to define my terms) has sometimes argued that he has a wider spread than I since he has written a book about God and I have not. There is a demurrer to that: I could write a book about God by merely digging out that thesis on Kant, and I have written verse whereas Elmer admits that he has not. Be that as it may, a bibliography of my work would stretch a considerable distance — from *Liberty* to the *Psychoanalytic Quarterly*, from coterie magazines of the fragrant Twenties which were issued in editions of thirty-two on hand-made paper to their principal emetic *The Saturday Evening Post*, from the program of the Harvard-Yale game to the confidential reports of *Consumer's Research*, from the private annals of the Social Science Research Council to the throwaways of a good many agitations. I have even appeared in the *New Republic*.

We have not discovered the specific Harvard-Yale program. The confidential reports of *Consumer's Research*
and the private annals of the Social Science Research
Council were not found, neither were various unsigned
articles written for government publications relating to
the National Parks and conservation. Furthermore, there
are constant allusions in DeVoto's correspondence to articles, reviews, and editorials which he has written but
which could not be traced. The editors of *Look* have no
records of ever publishing a DeVoto article and yet there
are references in the correspondence to such articles:
"*Look* just sent me $750.00 on the 'Martini' piece"; "I
am doing a slight but useful piece for *Look*"; "*Look* wants
a piece on the Forest Service"; and "The enclosed copy of
my *Look* piece." There are also references to newspaper
articles: "I covered baseball games for the Ogden Standard
(or Ogden Evening Standard) in addition to an embryonic
sports column. I covered local Chautauqua and sometimes
did the hotels or court house or what not when Lennie had
something else to do"; "I hung around the *Tribune*, wrote
verses lampooning the President of the University — and
I must have written other stuff"; and again, ". . . while I
was at Harvard I occasionally wrote some stuff for the
Boston *Herald*."

This bibliography does not pretend to be a complete,
definitive description of the works of Bernard DeVoto.
We have added to the short selective checklist compiled
by Garrett Mattingly and published in 1938 in *Bernard
DeVoto; A Preliminary Appraisal* and to Robert Edson

Lee's unpublished doctoral dissertation, "The Work of Bernard DeVoto; Introduction and Annotated Checklist." The present work contains many additions and corrections to the checklist published by Stanford University in 1960. We intend the present bibliography to be a useful guide to the student and scholar and hope that in years to come a more definitive bibliography can be compiled which will add to the present list the ephemeral items that appeared in newspapers, government publications, and "throwaways."

There are a few general statements to be made regarding this bibliography. Biographical, critical, and bibliographical books on DeVoto are not listed. To date there are no selective or collective publications of DeVoto's works. The first four sections are arranged in chronological order. Three unpublished major works are listed at the end of Section A. All other unpublished works are listed in Section E. Complete description including collation has not been attempted. DeVoto wrote articles anonymously and under the following pseudonyms: Cady Hewes, C. H., John August, J. A., Frank Gilbert, Fairley Blake, and Richard Dye. Articles written under a pseudonym are so noted.

The thoughtfulness of Mrs. DeVoto and her sons has added his personal papers to the public domain. They were purchased by Stanford University from his estate in May, 1956, with money from the William Robertson Coe Fund and a most generous gift from Mr. and Mrs. Edward H. Heller of Atherton, California. The good offices of Professor and Mrs. Wallace E. Stegner of Stanford and their close friendship with Mr. and Mrs. DeVoto made the acquisition of the collection possible. The original purchase has been augmented by gifts from forty-two individuals and publications. The papers were opened for public use in the spring of 1959. They number over 40,000 items and include the large majority of the known existing DeVoto manuscripts and almost forty years of DeVoto's correspondence. There are also research notes, photographs, annotated maps, biographical data, and memorabilia. Stanford ownership of the original manuscript or typescript copy is noted in the description of the individual work in this bibliography.

DeVoto's library of 5000 volumes was purchased from his estate at the same time as the papers. It reflects his catholicity of thought and scholarly judgment. Until such time as it becomes the core of a proposed library of American civilization, the books have been catalogued for use in various sections of the Stanford Library system.

Many people are due thanks for their help in the compilation of data, checking entries and copy, and correcting errors. They include Blaine M. Simons and Mrs. Helen H. Riser of Salt Lake City, Carl Bridenbaugh of the University of California at Berkeley, several members of the staff of the Stanford Library, particularly Dorothy Schoenberger, Betty H. Dutton, Lise Giraud, Philip W. Tarter, and Eric A. Thompson of the Division of Special Collections, and Dale L. Morgan, of the Bancroft Library at Berkeley, who read the entire manuscript and noted many errors and omissions.

Grateful acknowledgment is made to the editors and staff of the periodicals listed below. They have aided the compilers by checking their records for accurate data concerning the publication of DeVoto's works. They are: *Authors League Bulletin; American Heritage; American Association of University Professors Bulletin; American Mercury; Proceedings* of the American Philosophical Society; *The American Scholar; Chicago Sun-Times; Cosmopolitan; Current History; Esquire; Ford Times; Fortune; Good Housekeeping; Harper's Magazine;* the History Book Club *Review; Improvement Era; Jewish Frontier; The Lamp; Lincoln and Mercury Times; Look; Mademoiselle; Middlebury College News Letter; National Geographic Magazine; New York Herald Tribune; The New York Times; Reader's Digest; Redbook Magazine; The Saturday Evening Post; Saturday Review; True; The Twainian; The University of Colorado Bulletin; Woman's Day;* and *The Writer.* Carl D. Brandt, W. Colston Leigh, and Curtis Brown, Ltd., former literary agents for DeVoto, have checked our listing against their files.

The compilers are primarily grateful to Robert Edson Lee of the University of Colorado. His careful and thorough dissertation is the basis for the present bibliography as it was for the checklist published by Stanford. Lee's checklist of "The Easy Chair" essays (noted in Section C of this bibliography) has been of enormous aid in sorting out the problems engendered by their titles. (It should be said here that DeVoto had penciled in titles to five Easy Chairs in his own bound copies, copies to which Lee did not have access when he examined the DeVoto Papers at Stanford and to which he did not therefore refer in his checklist.)

The interest of Mrs. DeVoto and Professor Stegner in this undertaking has been of invaluable aid. A tremendous debt of gratitude is due Elaine Parnie who compiled and arranged the data for Sections C, D, and E. Our sincere appreciation is extended to the Stanford Library Administrators who made it possible for us to accomplish this work.

Any errors in this bibliography are the sole responsibility of the undersigned.

JULIUS P. BARCLAY

A. Books

T HIS section includes translations, foreign and variant editions, and reprints. Although the first edition of every major work as well as those variant editions and translations which are a part of the Stanford holdings are described, no attempt has been made to locate and describe all editions of each work. Included here are descriptions of the serial, drama, and lecture forms. These are also noted in the appropriate sections for serials, lectures, and so forth. The pagination is simply a notation of the pages, numbered and unnumbered, preceding page 1 and those pages that follow page 1. Manuscript dedications and annotations which appear in the Stanford copy of the book are noted.

1. Published

A1 THE CROOKED MILE

THE CROOKED MILE / BY / BERNARD DEVOTO / [quotation in two lines] / [device] / NEW YORK / MINTON, BALCH AND COMPANY / 1924

iv, 432 pp. 19½ × 13 cm. Red paper boards lettered in black on the front cover and downward on the spine. (The DeVoto-Stanford copy contains a one-page inscription to DeVoto's father, Florian Bernard DeVoto, on the front end-paper dated Evanston, Illinois, 30 September, 1924.)

A2 THE CHARIOT OF FIRE

THE / CHARIOT OF FIRE / AN AMERICAN NOVEL / BY / BERNARD
DEVOTO / AUTHOR OF / THE CROOKED MILE / NEW YORK /
THE MACMILLAN COMPANY / 1926 / All rights reserved

vi, 356 pp. 19½ × 13½ cm. Black paper boards lettered
in green on the front cover and downward on the spine.
(The DeVoto-Stanford copy contains a one-page inscription to DeVoto's father, Florian Bernard DeVoto, on the
front end-paper dated Evanston, [Illinois] 7 October,
1926.)

The DeVoto Papers include the manuscript of the
novel which was first entitled "The Burning Bush." (See
E17.)

A3 THE HOUSE OF SUN-GOES-DOWN

THE / HOUSE OF SUN-GOES-DOWN / BY / BERNARD DEVOTO /
[quotation in four lines] / NEW YORK / THE MACMILLAN
COMPANY /1928 / All rights reserved

x, 408 pp. 19½ × 13½ cm. Black paper boards lettered
in green on the front cover and downward on the spine.
Orange pictorial dust jacket printed in black. (The
DeVoto-Stanford copy contains a one-page inscription to
DeVoto's father, Florian Bernard DeVoto, on the front
end-paper dated [Cambridge, Massachusetts] 2 May,
1928.)

The DeVoto Papers include the partial manuscript and
two typescript copies of the early version entitled "The
Third Generation."

A4 MARK TWAIN'S AMERICA

MARK TWAIN'S / AMERICA / BY BERNARD DEVOTO / [illustra-
tion] / ILLUSTRATED BY M. J. GALLAGHER / LITTLE, BROWN,
AND COMPANY / 1932

xviii, 353 pp. 24½ × 16½ cm. Blue cloth lettered in gold
on the front cover and downward on the spine. Orange
and brown pictorial dust jacket printed in white and

brown. (The DeVoto-Stanford copy contains a page from DeVoto's diary dated April 5, 1929, with the legend "Began 'Mark Twain: A Preface.' " which is tipped inside the front cover.)

The following notation is written on the front end-paper:

This copy is unique in that it is the only copy of the first printing in which the date of Mark Twain's birth is incorrectly given [November 13 instead of November 30] on page 26 — a printer's error, since the manuscript gave the correct date. All other copies have been made correct by the printing and insertion of a cancel.

September 10, 1932   ALFRED R. McINTYRE

The DeVoto Papers include the partial manuscript, the typescript, and the galley proof copies.

Other editions were published in 1933 by the Chautauqua Institution, Chautauqua, New York, and in 1951 by Houghton Mifflin Company, Boston. Both were illustrated by M. J. Gallagher.

A5 WE ACCEPT WITH PLEASURE

WE ACCEPT / WITH PLEASURE / [rule] / BERNARD DEVOTO / [quotation in one line] / BOSTON, LITTLE, BROWN, AND COMPANY 1934 [border ornaments at the top and bottom of the page]

viii, 471 pp. 22½ × 14½ cm. Blue cloth stamped in gold on the front cover and spine and lettered in gold downward on the spine. Blue and brown dust jacket printed in white.

The DeVoto Papers include the manuscript.

(A part of the original manuscript entitled "Second Gentleman" is the property of Mrs. Madeline McQuown of San Jose, California.)

A6 FORAYS AND REBUTTALS

[nine rules] / FORAYS / [two rules] / AND REBUTTALS / [nine rules] / BERNARD DE VOTO / [nine rules] / PUBLISHED AT BOSTON IN 1936 BY / LITTLE, BROWN, AND COMPANY / [fifteen rules. The entire title page is enclosed by a continuous rule which is in turn enclosed by a border ornament.]

xiv, 403 pp. 23½ × 15 cm. Dark blue cloth stamped in gold on the front cover and spine and lettered downward on the spine. Green and gray dust jacket printed in blue.

Forays and Rebuttals is a collection of periodical articles and book reviews published between 1927 and 1936. One article "The Centennial of Mormonism" was expanded from *The American Mercury* for January, 1930. To the reprinted essays two addresses have been added: "Mark Twain: The Ink of History" and "Mark Twain and the Limits of Criticism." (See D2 and D3.)

A7 TROUBLED STAR

TROUBLED / STAR / [wavy rule] / BY / JOHN AUGUST / [device] / [rule] / BOSTON / LITTLE, BROWN AND COMPANY / 1939

iv, 310 pp. 20 × 13½ cm. Black paper boards lettered in red on the front cover and downward on the spine.

Troubled Star was published serially in *Collier's* in volume 102 in the issues of September 3–November 5, 1938.

A8 RAIN BEFORE SEVEN

RAIN / BEFORE SEVEN / BY JOHN AUGUST / [device] / BOSTON / LITTLE, BROWN AND COMPANY. 1940

iv, 280 pp. 21 × 14 cm. Blue cloth lettered in red on the front cover and downward on the spine. Green and purple pictorial dust jacket printed in white, yellow and beige.

Rain Before Seven was published serially in *Collier's* in volume 105 in the issues of May 25–July 27, 1940.

A9 MINORITY REPORT

[wavy rule] / MINORITY / REPORT / [wavy rule] / BERNARD
DEVOTO / [device] / PUBLISHED AT BOSTON IN 1940 BY /
LITTLE, BROWN AND COMPANY

x, 346 pp. 22½ × 14¾ cm. Blue cloth stamped in gold on
the front cover and spine and lettered downward on the
spine. Blue dust jacket printed in white.

Minority Report is a collection of articles reprinted
from *Harper's Magazine* and the *Saturday Review of
Literature*.

A10 MARK TWAIN AT WORK

MARK TWAIN / AT WORK / BY / BERNARD DEVOTO / [de-
vice] / CAMBRIDGE MASSACHUSETTS / HARVARD UNIVERSITY
PRESS / 1942. [The title page is enclosed by a continuous
rule which is in turn enclosed by a border ornament.]

xiv, 144 pp. Frontispiece (portrait), 2 facsimiles, 24½ ×
15¾ cm. Green cloth lettered in gold downward on the
spine. Dust jacket printed in black and white with a
photograph of Mark Twain on the front cover.

"The Symbols of Despair" was the William Vaughn
Moody Lecture at the University of Chicago in March,
1940. (See D8.) "The Phantasy of Boyhood" and "Noon
and the Dark" were printed as introductions to editions
of *Tom Sawyer* and *Huckleberry Finn* published by the
Limited Editions Club. (See B12 and B16.)

A11 ADVANCE AGENT

ADVANCE AGENT / BY JOHN AUGUST / [device] / BOSTON /
LITTLE, BROWN AND COMPANY. 1942

iv, 277 pp. 20½ × 13½ cm. Beige cloth stamped *J A* on
the front cover and lettered downward on the spine. Pictorial dust jacket printed in white and blue.

The DeVoto Papers include an annotated typescript
and the final typescript copy.

Advance Agent was published serially in *Collier's* in volume 108 in the issues of July 5–August 30, 1941.

Another edition published by Popular Library, New York, N.Y. [n.d.]. No. 133 in the Popular Library paper-back series.

English edition: ADVANCE AGENT / BY / JOHN AUGUST / SELWYN & BLOUNT, LTD. / LONDON / [1942]
> 140 pp. 18¾ × 12½ cm. Red cloth lettered in black on the spine. Pictorial dust jacket printed in red, blue, black, and green.

Spanish translation: JOHN AUGUST / AGENTE DE AVANZADA / TRADUCCIÓN DE M. TERUGGI / [device] / EDITORIAL CALOMINO / CALLE 49–660 — LA PLATA [ARGENTINA]
> 265, iv pp. 18 × 12 cm. Paper bound. Green and yellow dust jacket printed in black.
> On verso of title page: Copyright 1945.

A12 THE YEAR OF DECISION

THE YEAR OF / DECISION / 1846 [above surrounded by a design and surmounted by an eagle] / BY / BERNARD DEVOTO / [wavy rule] / BOSTON: / LITTLE, BROWN AND COMPANY / 1943
> xx, 524 pp. 22½ × 15 cm. Blue cloth lettered in brown on the front cover and downward on the spine. Pictorial dust jacket, blue background printed in red, yellow, black, and white. Front and back end-papers are maps of the western United States.
> On verso of title page: Copyright 1942, 1943 . . . [Published March 1943]
> (The above description is a Book of the Month Club edition. The first edition, which is not represented in the DeVoto–Stanford Collection, is a large paper edition bound in blue cloth with red lettering. On the verso of the title page the following notation appears: "First edition. Published March 1943.")

The DeVoto Papers include the manuscript and type-script copies.

DeVoto used material which he had gathered for *The Year of Decision* in a series of eight lectures given for the Lowell Institute in Boston in November and December of 1941. The series was entitled "American Empire, 1846: Manifest Destiny and the Western Frontier." (See D9.) The DeVoto Papers include an annotated typescript of the lectures.

Prior to publication by Little, Brown, portions of *The Year of Decision* were published in *The Atlantic Monthly*. They appeared in volume CLXX, in the issues for July, 1942 (pp. 77–94); August (pp. 79–94); September (pp. 111–126); October (pp. 113–125); November (pp. 109–125). The articles are divided into forty untitled chapters numbered consecutively, chapters which do not have any relationship to the chapters in the first edition. (See C456.)

Reprinted in a large paper edition in April, 1943, by Little, Brown and Company.

xx, 538 pp. 24½ × 16 cm. The binding and the dust jacket are identical to the March edition.

On verso of title page: Copyright 1942, 1943, . . . Published March 1943. Reprinted April 1943 . . .

Other editions were published in 1950 and 1961 by Houghton Mifflin Company, Boston. The 1961 paper-back edition contains an introduction by Catherine Drinker Bowen. The Introduction is the address which Mrs. Bowen gave at Stanford on October 1, 1960, and which is again printed in the present work.

German translation: BERNARD DEVOTO / DAS JAHR / DER ENTSCHEIDUNG / 1846 / [device] / WIEN / IM PHÖNIX VERLAG MCMLVIII [Translated by Dr. Adolph and Sophie Pichler]

xx, 660 pp. 21½ × 15½ cm. 1 folding map bound in.

Blue paper boards on front and back cover. Map of the United States stamped in gilt on the front cover and red cloth spine stamped in gilt and lettered downward on the spine.

On verso of title page: . . . Copyright 1948 by Wiener Phönix Verlag . . .

A13 THE LITERARY FALLACY

[rule] / BERNARD DEVOTO / [wavy rule] / THE LITERARY FALLACY / [device] / LITTLE, BROWN AND COMPANY. BOSTON / 1944

xii, 175 pp. 19¾ × 13 cm. Blue cloth lettered in gold downward on the spine.

On verso of title page: Copyright 1944 . . . First edition published April 1944 . . .

This volume comprises a reworking of five lectures which were delivered by DeVoto in March, 1943, at the University of Indiana under the auspices of the Patten Foundation. (See D15.)

A14 THE WOMAN IN THE PICTURE

THE WOMAN / IN THE PICTURE / BY JOHN AUGUST / [device] / BOSTON / LITTLE, BROWN AND COMPANY. 1944

vi, 265 pp. 19½ × 13 cm. Purple cloth stamped in gilt on the front cover and lettered downward on the spine.

On verso of title page: Copyright, . . . First edition published March 1944.

The Woman in the Picture was published serially in *Collier's* in volume 113 in the issues of January 8–29, 1944.

Abridged edition by Popular Library, New York, N.Y. [n.d.]. No. 65 in the Popular Library Mystery paper-back series.

English edition: THE WOMAN IN THE / PICTURE / BY / JOHN AUGUST / [device] / SELWYN & BLOUNT, LTD. / LONDON: : NEW YORK: : MELBOURNE / [1944]

144 pp. 19 × 12½ cm. Red cloth lettered in black downward on the spine. Pictorial dust jacket printed in blue, black, and red.

A15 ACROSS THE WIDE MISSOURI

ACROSS THE WIDE MISSOURI / BY / BERNARD DEVOTO / ILLUSTRATED WITH PAINTINGS BY / ALFRED JACOB MILLER, / CHARLES BODMER AND GEORGE CATLIN / WITH AN ACCOUNT OF THE DISCOVERY / OF THE MILLER COLLECTION BY / MAE REED PORTER / [device] / PUBLISHED BY HOUGHTON MIFFLIN COMPANY BOSTON / THE RIVERSIDE PRESS CAMBRIDGE MCMXLVII

xxviii, 483 pp. 81 plates, 25 × 17 cm. Tan cloth lettered in red on the front cover and downward on the spine. Front and back end-papers are a map of the fur trade country.

The DeVoto Papers include the manuscript, typescript, and an uncorrected proof copy.

Another limited edition of two hundred and sixty-five numbered copies autographed by the author was printed at the Riverside Press, Cambridge, for Houghton Mifflin in September, 1947. The DeVoto-Stanford copy is Number Two. This edition differs from the edition described above in two details. A leaf describing the edition has been inserted between the front end-paper and the first printed page. The book is bound in red cloth with a gilt figure on horseback on the front cover and a black label lettered in gold on the spine.

A16 MOUNTAIN TIME

MOUNTAIN TIME / BERNARD DEVOTO [enclosed by a continuous rule which is in turn enclosed by a border ornament] / LITTLE, BROWN AND COMPANY BOSTON 1947

vi, 313 pp. 20½ × 14 cm. Green paper-covered boards lettered in green on the front cover and in green and gold downward on the spine. Red and green dust jacket printed in black and white.

On verso of title page: Copyright 1946, 1947 . . .
[Published January 1947]

The DeVoto Papers include two manuscript and four typescript versions; one of the typescripts is a printer's copy and one is for *Collier's*. The early version was entitled "Everybody Got to Walk." The papers also include a radio script of *Mountain Time* with photographs of the actors. (See D49.)

Prior to publication by Little, Brown, *Mountain Time* was published in *Collier's*. It appeared in 1946 in volume 117, numbers 5–9, in the issues for February 2 (pp. 11–13+); February 9 (pp. 20–21+); February 16 (pp. 30–48); February 23 (pp. 17+); and March 2 (pp. 18+).

Reprinted in 1947 by Little, Brown and Company.
x, 357 pp. 20½ × 14 cm. Tan cloth lettered in red on the front cover and in red and gold downward on the spine.

On verso of title page: Copyright 1946, 1947 . . . First edition. Published January 1947 . . .

English edition: MOUNTAIN TIME / BY / BERNARD DEVOTO / LONDON / HAMMOND, HAMMOND & CO. LTD. / 87 GOWER STREET, W. C. I

[8] 316 pp. 20½ × 14 cm. Red cloth lettered in gold on the front cover and downward on the spine. Pictorial dust jacket printed in red, green, and black.

On verso of title page: Copyright . . . 1949.

A17 THE WORLD OF FICTION

THE / WORLD / OF FICTION   [rule] / BY BERNARD DEVOTO / [rule] / [device] / HOUGHTON MIFFLIN COMPANY · BOSTON / THE RIVERSIDE PRESS CAMBRIDGE

xiv, 299 pp. 21 × 14 cm. Red and blue cloth lettered in blue on the front cover and downward on the spine. Brown pictorial dust jacket printed in blue, black, and white.

On verso of title page: Copyright, 1950 . . .

The DeVoto Papers include three annotated type-script copies.

A18 THE HOUR

THE / HOUR / [rule] / BERNARD DEVOTO / HOUGHTON MIF-FLIN COMPANY BOSTON / THE RIVERSIDE PRESS CAMBRIDGE / 1951

x, 84 pp. illustrated, 21 × 14 cm. Gray and red cloth. Stamped in gold on the front cover and lettered in gold on the spine. Pictorial dust jacket printed in blue and pink.

On verso of title page: Copyright 1948, 1949, 1951 . . .

Chapter I "The American Spirits" was rewritten from the *Harper's Magazine* "The Easy Chair" for April, 1951, entitled "Whiskey Is for Patriots." Chapter II "For the Wayward and Beguiled" was written from "The Easy Chair" for December, 1949, published under the same title. Chapter III "The Enemy" was rewritten from "The Easy Chair" for March, 1948, entitled "Drinking Made Whimsical." (See also C706.)

The DeVoto Papers include the corrected typescript.

Reprinted in [1951] by Houghton Mifflin with illustrations by William Barss. Otherwise identical in size, pagination, format, and cover to first issue.

A19 THE COURSE OF EMPIRE

THE COURSE / OF EMPIRE / BY / BERNARD DEVOTO / WITH MAPS BY ERWIN RAISZ / [device] / HOUGHTON MIFFLIN COM-PANY BOSTON / THE RIVERSIDE PRESS CAMBRIDGE / 1952

xxii, 647 pp. 23 maps, 22 × 14½ cm. Gray cloth lettered in red on the front cover and downward on the spine. Pictorial dust jacket printed in white. Front and back end-papers are a relief map of the United States printed in brown and black as are all of the maps in the book. (The

DeVoto-Stanford copy is annotated by DeVoto in red ink.)

On verso of title page: Copyright, 1951, . . .

The DeVoto Papers include the manuscript and five typescript copies, two galley proofs and two copies of the unbound book, each copy with notes.

Stanford has three additional issues printed in 1952 by Houghton Mifflin:

a) THE COURSE / OF EMPIRE / BY / BERNARD DEVOTO / WITH MAPS BY ERWIN RAISZ / [device] / HOUGHTON MIFFLIN COMPANY BOSTON / THE RIVERSIDE PRESS CAMBRIDGE

Identical in size, pagination, and format with the first issue. Bound in blue cloth with red lettering.

b) THE COURSE (green ink) / OF EMPIRE (green) / BY / BERNARD DEVOTO / WITH MAPS BY ERWIN RAISZ / [device] (green) / HOUGHTON MIFFLIN COMPANY BOSTON

Identical in size, pagination, and format with the first issue. Bound in black with gold lettering. The end-paper maps and all of the maps in the back are printed in green and black.

c) Identical to b) above except for binding. Bound in red and green cloth with gold lettering.

English edition: WESTWARD THE / COURSE OF EMPIRE / BY / BERNARD DEVOTO / WITH MAPS BY ERWIN RAISZ / EYRE & SPOTTISWOODE / LONDON 1953

xxii, 647 pp. 23 maps, 22 × 14½ cm. Blue cloth lettered in gold downward on the spine. Gray dust jacket printed in red and black. Front and back end-papers are a relief map of the United States printed in brown and black, as are all the maps in the book.

A20 THE EASY CHAIR

THE / EASY CHAIR / BY / BERNARD DEVOTO / HOUGHTON MIFFLIN COMPANY BOSTON / THE RIVERSIDE PRESS CAMBRIDGE / 1955 xii, 356 pp. 22 × 15 cm. White and green marbled paper and black cloth lettered in gold on the spine. Yellow dust jacket printed in black and white with a photograph of DeVoto on the front cover.

On verso of title page: Copyright 1945, 1946, 1947, 1948, 1949, 1950, 1951, 1952, 1953, 1954, 1955.

Pages ix and x of the preface note that twenty-four of the thirty-one items reprinted here were "The Easy Chair" articles in *Harper's Magazine;* six were text articles in *Harper's;* and one appeared in the *Atlantic Monthly.*

The DeVoto Papers include an annotated typescript and the final typescript copy.

A21 WOMEN AND CHILDREN FIRST

WOMEN AND CHILDREN / FIRST / BY CADY HEWES / (Bernard DeVoto) / [rule] / HOUGHTON MIFFLIN COMPANY BOSTON / THE RIVERSIDE PRESS CAMBRIDGE / 1956

vi, 151 pp. 21 × 14½ cm. Blue paper, dark blue label on the spine lettered in gold. Blue, black, and pink dust jacket printed in blue, black, and white. Blue end-papers.

On verso of title page: Copyright 1949, 1950, 1951, 1952, 1953, 1954, 1955 . . . First printing November, 1956.

The articles in this book are reprinted by permission of *Woman's Day* magazine. Eleven of the articles appeared under the name Cady Hewes. Two of them "Homicide in the Home" and "The Life and Wife of a Writer" were written under DeVoto's name.

II. Unpublished

A22 COCK CROW

"Cock Crow," a novel. Completed about 1924.

The DeVoto Papers include a corrected typescript and the final typescript draft. Pages 1–174 of the original typescript is entitled "The Winged Man."

A23 ASSORTED CANAPES

"Assorted Canapes," a novel. Completed about 1954.
The DeVoto Papers include the partial manuscript and a typescript draft.

A24 WESTERN PARADOX

"Western Paradox," a volume concerned with the civilization and culture of the twentieth century American West. Completed about 1955.
The DeVoto Papers include the unfinished manuscript and a typescript draft.

B. Books and Periodicals Edited, or with Contributions, by Bernard DeVoto

EDITORIAL columns are noted in this section but they are listed as separate entries in *Section C*.

B1 OGDEN: THE UNDERWRITERS OF SALVATION

THE TAMING OF THE FRONTIER . . . Edited by Duncan Aikman. New York, Minton, Balch and Company, 1925.
"Ogden: The Underwriters of Salvation" by Bernard DeVoto, pp. 25–60.

(Reprinted in part as "Sin Comes to Ogden," pp. 446–454, in *Among the Mormons; Historical Accounts by Contemporary Observers*, edited by William Mulder and A. Russell Mortensen. Knopf, New York, 1958.)

The DeVoto Papers include two other articles entitled "Ogden." (See C818 and E89.)

B2 THE WRITER'S HANDBOOK

THE WRITER'S HANDBOOK. A MANUAL OF ENGLISH COMPOSITION.

By W. F. Bryan, Arthur H. Nethercot, Bernard DeVoto
. . . New York, The Macmillan Company, 1928.
"DeVoto's individual work is the chapter on 'Diction,' but all three authors worked together on the entire book, a rewrite of a previous text by W. F. Bryan." (Robert Edson Lee, "The Work of Bernard DeVoto, Introduction and Annotated Checklist," State University of Iowa doctoral dissertation, 1957.)

B3 THE CO-EDS: GOD BLESS THEM!

COLLEGE READINGS IN CONTEMPORARY THOUGHT. Selected and edited by Kendall Taft, John Francis McDermott, and Dana O. Jensen. Boston, Houghton Mifflin Company, 1929. "The Co-Eds: God Bless Them!" by Bernard DeVoto, pp. 234–246. (See C99.)

B4 THE LIFE AND ADVENTURES OF JAMES P. BECKWOURTH

THE LIFE AND ADVENTURES OF JAMES P. BECKWOURTH. Edited by T. D. Bonner. New York, Alfred A. Knopf, 1931. Americana Deserta Series. Edited, with a preface and introduction, by Bernard DeVoto. Preface by Bernard DeVoto, pp. ix–x; introduction pp. xix–xl.

The DeVoto Papers contain an unpublished article entitled "James P. Beckwourth" dated 1927. It was not incorporated in the introduction to this volume.

DeVoto was also the general editor of the Americana Deserta Series, published by Knopf. The following volumes were published:
a) Herman Melville. *Pierre or the Ambiguities.* Edited by Robert S. Forsyth. 1930.
b) *Tall Tales of the Southwest. An Anthology of Southern and Southwestern Humor 1830–1860.* Edited by Franklin J. Meine. 1930.

c) *The Genteel Female. An Anthology.* Edited by Clifton J. Furness. 1931.

d) James Fenimore Cooper. *The American Democrat.* Edited by H. L. Mencken. 1931.

e) Timothy Flint. *Recollections of the Last Ten Years.* Edited, with an introduction, by C. Hartley Grattan. 1932.

f) N. B. Tucker. *The Partisan Leaders.* Edited by Carl Bridenbaugh. 1933.

B5 FROM A GRADUATE'S WINDOW

HARVARD GRADUATES' MAGAZINE. The editor's column was entitled "From a Graduate's Window." DeVoto was the editor from September, 1930, to June, 1932, for eight issues. These are noted in *Section C.*

DeVoto also published four articles and two book reviews of his own in the *Harvard Graduates' Magazine* during the period of his editorship. One other article "Byron Satterlee Hurlbut" was published in March, 1930. These are noted in *Section C.*

B6 JOSEPH SMITH

DICTIONARY OF AMERICAN BIOGRAPHY. Edited by Dumas Malone. New York, Charles Scribner's Sons, 1935.

"Joseph Smith" by Bernard DeVoto, vol. XVII, pp. 310–312.

B7 BRIGHAM YOUNG

DICTIONARY OF AMERICAN BIOGRAPHY. Edited by Dumas Malone. New York, Charles Scribner's Sons, 1936.

"Brigham Young" by Bernard DeVoto, vol. XX, pp. 620–623.

B8 REVIEWING REVIEWS

SATURDAY REVIEW OF LITERATURE. Bernard DeVoto was the editor from September 26, 1936, to March 1, 1938. While editor, DeVoto wrote a column entitled "Reviewing Reviews" which appeared fifteen times between September 26, 1936, and December 4, 1937. These columns, together with other articles and editorials written by DeVoto, are noted in *Section C.*

B9 INTERRELATIONS OF HISTORY
AND LITERATURE
APPROACHES TO AMERICAN SOCIAL HISTORY. Edited by William E. Lingelbach. New York, D. Appleton-Century Company [c. 1937]. The Appleton-Century Historical Essays edited by William E. Lingelbach.
    "Interrelations of History and Literature" by Bernard DeVoto, pp. 34–56.

B10 ETHAN FROME
ETHAN FROME. By Edith Wharton. With an introduction by Bernard DeVoto. New York, Charles Scribner's Sons, 1938.
    Introduction by Bernard DeVoto, pp. v–xviii.
    The DeVoto Papers include a typescript copy.

B11 THE NOVELIST OF THE CATTLE KINGDOM
THE HIRED MAN ON HORSEBACK. MY STORY OF EUGENE MANLOVE RHODES. By May Davison Rhodes. Boston, Houghton Mifflin Company, 1938.
    Introduction: "The Novelist of the Cattle Kingdom" by Bernard DeVoto, pp. xix–xlix.
    The DeVoto Papers include a typescript copy.

B12 THE ADVENTURES OF TOM SAWYER
THE ADVENTURES OF TOM SAWYER. By Mark Twain. The text edited and with an introduction by Bernard DeVoto. Cambridge, Massachusetts, University Press, 1939. Printed for the members of the Limited Editions Club.
    Introduction by Bernard DeVoto. Reprinted in *A Book*

of Prefaces (see B15) and reprinted with changes in *Mark Twain at Work* under the title "The Phantasy of Boyhood." (See A10.)

B13 MARK TWAIN IN ERUPTION

MARK TWAIN IN ERUPTION. HITHERTO UNPUBLISHED PAGES ABOUT MEN AND EVENTS. By Mark Twain. Edited, and with an introduction, by Bernard DeVoto. New York, Harper and Brothers [1940].

Introduction by Bernard DeVoto, pp. vii–xxviii. (DeVoto was curator of the Mark Twain Papers from 1938 to 1946.)

B14 LEE FOSTER HARTMAN

LEE FOSTER HARTMAN, EDITOR OF HARPER'S MAGAZINE, 1931–1941. A resolution adopted by the Board of Directors of Harper and Brothers, October 20, 1941. Tributes from *Harper's Magazine* by Elmer Davis and Bernard DeVoto. New York, Harper and Brothers, 1941.

Essay: "Lee Foster Hartman" by Bernard DeVoto, pp. 15–26. (Reprinted from *Harper's Magazine*, "The Easy Chair" for December, 1941.) (See C446.)

B15 A PREFACE TO THE ADVENTURES OF TOM SAWYER

A BOOK OF PREFACES. Van Wyck Brooks and others. With a footnote by Sinclair Lewis. New York, The Limited Editions Club, 1941.

"A Preface to *The Adventures of Tom Sawyer*" by Bernard DeVoto, pp. 62–77. (See B12.)

B16 ADVENTURES OF HUCKLEBERRY FINN

ADVENTURES OF HUCKLEBERRY FINN. [TOM SAWYER'S COMPANION.] By Mark Twain. Edited, with an introduction, by Bernard DeVoto. Illustrated by Thomas Hart Benton. New York, The Limited Editions Club, 1942.

Introduction by Bernard DeVoto, pp. ix–lxx.

Reprinted with changes in *Mark Twain at Work* under the title "Noon and the Dark." (See A10.)

B17 MARK TWAIN: THE ARTIST AS AMERICAN
THIS IS MY BEST. Edited by Whit Burnett. New York, Dial Press, 1942.
"Mark Twain: The Artist as American" by Bernard DeVoto, pp. 195–205. (Reprinted from *Mark Twain's America*, Chapter XII "The Artist as American," pp. 298–321.) (See A4.)

B18 PORTRAIT OF AMERICA
PORTRAIT OF AMERICA. Preface by Bernard DeVoto. Edited by Aimée Crane. New York, Hyperion Press [1945].
Preface by Bernard DeVoto, pp. I–IV.

B19 MARK TWAIN ABOUT THE JEWS
JEWISH FRONTIER ANTHOLOGY 1934–1944. Jewish Frontier Association, Inc., 1945.
"Mark Twain About the Jews" by Bernard DeVoto, pp. 177–181. Reprinted from *Jewish Frontier* for May, 1939. (See C397.)

B20 THE PORTABLE MARK TWAIN
THE PORTABLE MARK TWAIN. Edited by Bernard DeVoto. New York, The Viking Press, 1946.
Introduction by Bernard DeVoto, pp. 1–34.

B21 AMERICA IN BOOKS
AMERICA IN BOOKS. A monthly publication of the History Book Club. Edited by Bernard DeVoto from May, 1947, through May, 1948. The editorials and book reviews written by DeVoto while editor of *America in Books* are noted in *Section C*.

B22 THE VALLEY OF SHADOWS
THE VALLEY OF SHADOWS. By Francis Grierson. Edited by

Theodore Spencer. New York, Houghton Mifflin for the History Book Club, 1948.

Editor's note by Bernard DeVoto.

B23 A TREASURY OF WESTERN FOLKLORE

A TREASURY OF WESTERN FOLKLORE. Edited by B[enjamin] A[lbert] Botkin. Foreword by Bernard DeVoto. New York, Crown Publishers, c. 1951, 1955. [Third printing, March, 1955.]

Foreword by Bernard DeVoto, pp. vii–xiv.

(The first edition did not contain the foreword written by DeVoto.)

B24 STRANGE EMPIRE

STRANGE EMPIRE. By Joseph Kinsey Howard. New York, William Morrow and Company, 1952.

Foreword "Joseph Kinsey Howard" by Bernard DeVoto, pp. 3–10.

B25 THE JOURNALS OF LEWIS AND CLARK

THE JOURNALS OF LEWIS AND CLARK. Edited by Bernard DeVoto. Maps by Erwin Raisz. Boston, Houghton Mifflin Company [c. 1953].

Preface by Bernard DeVoto, pp. v–x. Introduction by Bernard DeVoto, pp. xv–lii.

The DeVoto Papers include the corrected and the final typescript copies.

English edition: THE JOURNALS OF LEWIS AND CLARK. Edited by Bernard DeVoto. Maps by Erwin Raisz. London, Eyre and Spottiswoode, 1954.

B26 BEYOND THE HUNDREDTH MERIDIAN

BEYOND THE HUNDREDTH MERIDIAN. JOHN WESLEY POWELL AND THE SECOND OPENING OF THE WEST. By Wallace Stegner.

With an introduction by Bernard DeVoto. Boston, Houghton Mifflin [c. 1953, 1954].
Introduction by Bernard DeVoto, pp. xv–xxiii.

B27 TIMBER IN YOUR LIFE
TIMBER IN YOUR LIFE. By Arthur H. Carhart. Introduction by Bernard DeVoto. Philadelphia, J. B. Lippincott Company, 1955 [c. 1954].
Introduction by Bernard DeVoto, pp. 7–19.

B28 THE ONE-EYED POACHER AND THE MAINE WOODS
THE ONE-EYED POACHER AND THE MAINE WOODS. By Edmund Ware Smith. With an introduction by Bernard DeVoto. New York, Frederick Fell, Inc., 1955.
Introduction by Bernard DeVoto, pp. 9–14.
The DeVoto Papers include a typescript copy.

B29 THE COEDS WERE REAL — THE BOYS WERE SHADOWS
THE COLLEGE YEARS. Edited by A[uguste] C. Spectorsky. New York, Hawthorn Books, Inc. [1958].
"The Co-Eds Were Real — The Boys Were Shadows" by Bernard DeVoto, pp. 490–495. Originally printed in *College Humor* in 1929. (See C128.)

B30 THE AMERICAN ROAD
FREEDOM OF THE AMERICAN ROAD. Edited by William Laas. [Detroit] Ford Motor Company, n.d.
"The American Road" by Bernard DeVoto, pp. 7–8.

B31 YELLOWSTONE NATIONAL PARK
THE GLORY OF OUR WEST. Introduction by Joseph Henry Jackson. San Carlos, Calif., Nourse, 1958. (The editors have not seen a copy of the first edition which was published by Doubleday and Company in 1952.)
"Yellowstone National Park" by Bernard DeVoto, p. 32.

C. Contributions to Periodicals

SHORT STORIES, editorials, letters to the editor, and book reviews are identified and reference is made to reprinted articles. Fiction, essays, and editorials published in serial form, such as "English '37," are noted in their entirety under the date of the first issue. Articles and editorials with the same title which were not published in serial form, such as "Reviewing Reviews," are listed separately. The name and volume number and the date of the periodical in which the article appeared and the pagination of each item are given. The titles of The Easy Chair essays presented special problems and reference has been made to the admirably compiled listing by Robert Edson Lee printed in the *Bulletin of Bibliography and Magazine Notes*, Volume 23, Number 3 for September–December, 1960, "The Easy Chair Essays of Bernard DeVoto: A Finding List." The following abbreviations have been used throughout:

Chicago Post: The Chicago Evening Post Literary Review

Evanston: The Evanston News-Index

Harper's: Harper's Magazine

Harvard: The Harvard Graduates' Magazine

NEQ: The New England Quarterly

NYHT Book: The New York Herald Tribune Weekly Book Review

NYT Book: The New York Times Book Review

Post: The Saturday Evening Post

SRL: The Saturday Review of Literature (later Saturday Review)

W Day: Woman's Day

The asterisk (*) denotes a manuscript or typescript copy in the DeVoto Papers.

1913

*C1 "The Reasonableness of World-wide Conciliation," *Ogden Standard* (May 10).

1914

C2 "The Doctor," *The University Pen*, vol. 1 (December), 65–74. Short story. Reprinted in a special anniversary issue [1947] of the University of Utah literary magazine *Pen*, 22–23+.

1924

C3 "Children Best Part of Novel," *Evanston* (December 16), 7. Review of Mrs. Edward (Mary Borden) Spears, *Three Pilgrims and a Tinker*.

C4 "Lesion," *The Guardian* I (December), 4–7. Short story.

C5 "America by the Frontier Formula," *Chicago Post* (December 26), 8. Review of Frederic L. Paxson, *History of the American Frontier*.

C6 "An American Tragedy," *SRL* I (December 27), 412. Review of Stewart Edward White, *The Glory Hole*.

1925

C7 "An Inconclusive Symposium," *Chicago Post* (January 16), 5. Review of Malcolm R. Thorpe, editor, *Organic Adaptation to Environment*.

C8 "Sees Paradox in Duel with Vatican," *Evanston* (January 20), 7. Review of Alfred Loisy, *Duel with Vatican*.

C9 "Lake Land's Spell Lives in This Book," *Evanston* (January 27), 7. Review of Charles B. Reed, *Four-Way Lodge*.

C10 "Mencken Beheads Headless Corpses," *Evanston* (January 27), 7. Review of H. L. Mencken, *Prejudices, Fourth Series*.

C11 "This Is True Epic of American Land," *Evanston* (February 3), 7. Review of Mary Austin, *A Land of Journey's Ending.*

C12 "Paint Future in Sad, Glad Colors," *Evanston* (February 24), 7. Reviews of Gerald Heard, *Narcissus*, and F. C. S. Schiller, *Tantalus.*

C13 "God — Litterateur," *The Guardian* I (March), 188–197.

C14 "Digging up Literary Remains of Conrad," *Evanston* (March 3), 7. Review of Joseph Conrad, *Tales of Hearsay.*

C15 "Puts 'Arrowsmith' with Great Novels," *Evanston* (March 10), 7. Review of Sinclair Lewis, *Arrowsmith.*

C16 "Van Doren in Appraisal of J. B. Cabell," *Evanston* (March 17), 7. Review of Carl Van Doren, *James Branch Cabell.*

C17 "A Naturalist in Paradise," *Chicago Post* (March 20), 5. Review of Robert Cushman Murphy, *Bird Islands of Peru.*

C18 "The Science of History," *Chicago Post* (March 20), 6. Reviews of Jacques De Morgan, *Prehistoric Man*, and C. E. Fox, *The Threshold of the Pacific.*

C19 "Sin Comes to Brattle Street," *SRL* I (March 21), 611. Review of B. H. Lehman, *Wild Marriage.*

C20 "Blind Man's Buff Is Not Hémon's Best," *Evanston* (March 24), 9. Review of Louis Hémon, *Blind Man's Buff*, and Elmer Davis, *The Keys of the City.*

C21 "Perfect Comedian Is Aldous Huxley," *Evanston* (March 31), 15. Review of Aldous Huxley, *Those Barren Leaves.*

C22 "What Causes This Honing for Arcady?" *Evanston* (April 7), 7. Review of Robert Nathan, *Jonah.*

C23 "The Stop of Blood," *SRL* I (April 18), 687–688. Review of Percy Marks, *Martha.*

C24 "Writer Foresees Doom of Mankind," *Evanston* (April 21), 15. Review of Stanton H. Coblentz, *The Decline of Man.*

C25 "Scientists Show Secrets to Public," *Evanston* (April 28), 10. Reviews of F. G. Crookshank, *The Mongol in Our Midst*; J. B. S. Haldane, *Gallinicus*; and C. J. Patten, *The Passing of the Phantoms.*

C26 "Kreymborg Tells Tale of Moderns," *Evanston* (May 5), 7. Review of Alfred Kreymborg, *Troubadour.*

C27 "Ghosts as Social Assets," *Chicago Post* (May 8), 3. Review of Charles G. Harper, *Haunted Houses.*

C28 "On Making History an Exact Science," *Evanston* (May 19), 7. Review of Frederic L. Paxson, *A History of the American Frontier.*

C29 "Indoor Morality Outdoors," *Chicago Post* (May 22), 8. Review of Earle Amos Brooks, *A Handbook of the Outdoors.*

C30 "Ellen LaMotte Tells of Opium Trade in East," *Evanston* (May 26), 9. Review of Ellen LaMotte, *Snuffs and Butters.*

C31 "Adventures of a Scholar Tramp," *Evanston* (June 2), 7. Review of Glen H. Mullins, *Adventures of a Scholar Tramp.*

C32 "Frontier Days and Industrial Emergence," *Chicago Post* (June 5), 5. Review of Theodore Calvin Pease, *The Story of Illinois.*

C33 "Our First International Gentleman," *Chicago Post* (June 5), 2. Review of George S. Hellman, *Washington Irving, Esquire.*

C34 "Everything about Prehistoric Man," *Chicago Post* (June 12), 1. Review of George MacCurdy, *Human Origins.*

C35 "The Odyssey of Mormonism," *SRL* I (June 27), 853. Review of M. R. Werner, *Brigham Young.*

C36 "New and Old Poems by Mr. Nicholson," *Evanston* (August 11), 8. Reviews of J. U. Nicholson, *King of the Black Isles* and *The Drums of Yle.*

C37 "Is the New Woman Superior to Old?" *Evanston* (September 7), 5. Reviews of Anthony M. Ludovici, *Lysistrata, or Woman's Future and Future Woman,* and

Dora Russell, *Hypatia, or Woman and Knowledge*.

C38 " 'Prometheus' Seeks to Annihilate Bunk," *Evanston* (September 14), 5. Reviews of H. S. Jennings, *Prometheus;* Vernon Lee, *Proteus;* and H. F. Scott Stokes, *Perseus*.

C39 " 'Quo Vadimus' Tale of the Golden Age," *Evanston* (September 16), 5. Reviews of D'Albe, *Quo Vadimus*, and Wright, *The Conquest of Cancer*.

C40 "Timothy Dexter Was American Nobleman," *Evanston* (September 21), 5. Review of J. P. Marquand, *Lord Timothy Dexter*.

C41 "The Good Old Days — Best in Southwest," *Evanston* (September 30), 5. Review of Owen P. White, *Them Was the Days, from El Paso to Prohibition*.

C42 "Bojer's 'Emigrants' Fine Work of Art," *Evanston* (November 4), 8. Review of Johan Bojer, *The Emigrants*.

C43 "Here Is Genuine American Poetry," *Evanston* (November 18), 11. Review of John G. Neihardt, *The Song of the Indian Wars*.

C44 "Alexander Writes of Indian Dramas," *Evanston* (November 25), 8. Review of Hartley Alexander, *Manito Masks*.

C45 "Aaron Burr Is Vindicated," *Chicago Post* (November 27), 2. Review of Samuel H. Wandell and Meade Minnigerode, *Aaron Burr*.

C46 "Morale of Enemy Objective of War," *Evanston* (December 2), 8. Review of B. H. Liddell Hart, *Paris or the Future of War*.

C47 "Bercovici Writes of Melting Pot," *Evanston* (December 9), 10. Review of Conrad Bercovici, *On New Shores*.

C48 " 'Murder at Smutty Nose' Enthralling Book of Crime," *Evanston* (December 10), 36. Review of Edmund Pearson, *Murder at Smutty Nose*.

C49 " 'Prairie' Faithful to Midland Creed," *Evanston* (December 16), 8. Review of Walter J. Mullenburg, *Prairie*.

C50 "A Working Philosophy of Liberty," *Chicago Post* (December 18), 2. Review of Hendrik Van Loon, *Tolerance*.

C51 "Newton Produces a Literary Gem," *Evanston* (December 23), 7. Review of A. Edward Newton, *The Greatest Book in the World*.

C52 " 'First Forty-Niner' Story of the West," *Evanston* (December 30), 7. Review of James A. B. Scherer, *The First Forty-Niner*.

1926

C53 "Bertrand Russell on 'What I Believe,' " *Evanston* (January 6), 9. Review of Bertrand Russell, *What I Believe*.

C54 "American Husband Finds a Champion," *Evanston* (January 20), 9. Review of Alexander Black, *American Husbands*.

C55 "Hauptman Novel Joyous Allegory," *Evanston* (February 3), 5. Review of Gerhart Hauptman, *The Island of the Great Mother*.

C56 "Interpretation of Indians Pleasing," *Evanston* (February 10), 5. Review of Eda Lou Walton, *Dawn Boy*.

C57 "See Machine Age Bringing World Chaos," *Evanston* (February 10), 5. Review of Garet Garrett, *Ouroboros or the Mechanical Extension of Mankind*.

C58 "1925 Short Stories Disappoint Critic," *Evanston* (February 17), 5. Review of Edward J. O'Brien, editor, *The Best Short Stories of 1925*.

C59 "Reformer Writes Brilliant Document," *Evanston* (February 24), 5. Review of Frederick C. Howe, *The Confessions of a Reformer*.

C60 "Southwest Glorified by C. F. Lummis," *Evanston* (February 24), 5. Review of C. F. Lummis, *Mesa, Canon and Pueblo*.

*C61 "Utah," *American Mercury* VII (March), 317–323. (The DeVoto Papers include the annotated page proofs signed and dated 13 December 1925.)

C62 "Huxley Gives Dope about Traveling," *Evanston* (March 3), 5. Review of Aldous Huxley, *Along the Road*.

C63 "Your Future Morality Is Safe," *Evanston* (March 10), 10. Review of C. E. M. Joad, *Thrasymachus.*

C64 " 'The Oldest God' Is Robust Irony," *Evanston* (March 17), 10. Review of Stephen McKenna, *The Oldest God.*

C65 "Norris Shown Too Much Profundity," *Evanston* (March 24), 10. Review of Charles G. Norris, *Pig Iron.*

C66 "The Paradox of D. H. Lawrence," *Evanston* (March 24), 10. Review of D. H. Lawrence, *The Plumed Serpent.*

C67 "Memories of One Lucky American," *Evanston* (March 31), 21. Review of Walt McDougall, *This Is the Life.*

C68 "Mrs. Wembridge's Further Moronia," *Evanston* (March 31), 21. Review of Eleanor R. Wembridge, *Other Peoples' Daughters.*

C69 "Americana Vaunts Two Masterpieces," *Evanston* (April 7), 15. Reviews of Walter Noble Burns, *The Saga of Billy the Kid,* and George H. Devol, *Forty Years a Gambler on the Mississippi.*

C70 "Ammunition for an Attack on Babbitt," *Evanston* (April 21), 20. Review of Duncan Aikman, *The Home Town Mind.*

C71 "The Mauve Decade from Two Angles," *Evanston* (April 28), 24. Reviews of Thomas Beer, *The Mauve Decade,* and Floyd Dell, *Intellectual Vagabondage.*

C72 "Jurgen Performs in Cabell Novel," *Evanston* (May 5), 18. Review of James B. Cabell, *The Silver Stallion.*

C73 "Stribling Scores in 'Teeftallow,' " *Evanston* (May 5), 18. Review of T. S. Stribling, *Teeftallow.*

C74 "South Lambastes Minnigerode Book," *Evanston* (May 19), 21. Review of Meade Minnigerode, *Some American Ladies.*

C75 "A Critical Analysis of the Sacco-Vanzetti Case," *Evanston* (June 1), 10. Review of Felix Frankfurter, *The Case of Sacco and Vanzetti.*

C76 " 'Americana' Shelf Gets New Volume," *Evanston* (October 6), 17. Review of P. E. Byrne, *Soldiers of the Plains.*

C77 "Saving the Sophomore" by Richard Dye. *American Mercury* IX (November), 288–294.

C78 "Vestige of a Nordic Arcady," *American Mercury* IX (November), 327–332.

C79 "Mr. Nathan Gets Hilarious over the American Drama," *Evanston* (November 17), 7. Review of George Jean Nathan, *The House of Satan.*

C80 "Names 'Doctor's Memories' Year's Most Interesting," *Evanston* (November 24), 7. Review of Victor C. Vaughan, *A Doctor's Memories.*

C81 "The Mountain Men," *American Mercury* IX (December), 472–479.

C82 "Will James Gives West Its True Color and Loveliness," *Evanston* (December 1), 17. Review of Will James, *Smoky.*

C83 "Dr. Collins Treats Tabooed Subjects with Ripe Wisdom," *Evanston* (December 10), 20. Review of Joseph Collins, *The Doctor Looks at Love and Life.*

C84 " 'Wild Bill Hickok' Hastily Done but It Reads Well," *Evanston* (December 10), 40. Review of Frank J. Wilstach, *Wild Bill Hickok.*

1927

*C85 "College and the Exceptional Man," *Harper's* CLIV (January), 253–260.

C86 "Harry Kemp Exhibits His Life in Greenwich Village," *Evanston* (January 12), 8. Review of Harry Kemp, *More Miles.*

C87 " 'The Hard-boiled Virgin' Is Caviar for the Particular," *Evanston* (January 12), 8. Review of Frances Newman, *The Hard-boiled Virgin.*

C88 "Seitz's Book 'Dreadful' in Format," *Evanston* (February 2), 8. Review of Don C. Seitz, *The Dreadful Decade.*

C89 " 'The Delectable Mountains' Adds to Burt's Reputation," *Evanston* (February 2), 8. Review of Struthers Burt, *The Delectable Mountains.*

C90 "George Washington the Man Shown without Senti-
ment," *Evanston* (February 9), 8. Review of W. E.
Woodward, *George Washington, The Image and the
Man.*

C91 " 'Chevrons' Is Truth about American Army in France,"
Evanston (February 16), 7. Review of Leonard Mason,
Chevrons.

C92 "Sinclair Lewis Continues Progress in 'Elmer Gantry,' "
Evanston (March 16), 8. Review of Sinclair Lewis,
Elmer Gantry.

C93 "Asbury Writes Definitive History of Methodist Mind,"
Evanston (April 6), 10. Review of Herbert Asbury,
A Methodist Saint.

C94 " 'Revolt in the Desert' Is Destined for Immortality,"
Evanston (April 27), 10. Review of T. E. Lawrence,
Revolt in the Desert.

C95 "Figures and Events of 1926–7 Run in Review," *Evanston*
(May 11), 10. Review of Grant Overton, editor, *Mirrors of the Year.*

C96 "The Great Medicine Road," *American Mercury* XI
(May), 104–112.

C97 "The Argonaut Makes Its Debut," *Evanston* (June 8), 12.
Review of Arthur D. Howden Smith, editor, *The Narrative of Samuel Hancock.*

C98 "In Search of Bergamot," *Harper's* CLV (August), 302–
312. Short story.

C99 "The Co-Ed: The Hope of Liberal Education," *Harper's*
CLV (September), 452–459. Reprinted in *Forays and
Rebuttals* under the title "The Co-Eds: God Bless
Them," 240–256. Reprinted in *College Readings in
Contemporary Thought,* 234–236, edited by Kendall
Taft and others, Department of English, Washington
University. Boston, Houghton Mifflin Company, 1929.
(See B3.)

C100 "Footnote on the West," *Harper's* CLV (November),
713–722.

C101 "Front Page Ellen," *Redbook* L (November), 32–37+. Short story.

C102 "Sons of Martha," *SRL* IV (November 19), 321. Review of T. Morris Longstreth, *The Silent Force.*

*C103 "Sleeping Dogs," *Post* CC (November 19), 18–19+. Short story.

C104 "Casehardened Men," *SRL* IV (December 10), 426. Review of Walter Noble Burns, *Tombstone.*

C105 "A Social Experiment," *SRL* IV (December 24), 468. Review of Judge Ben B. Lindsey and Wainwright Evans, *The Companionate Marriage.*

1928

C106 "Farewell to Pedagogy," *Harper's* CLVI (January), 182–190. Reprinted in *Forays and Rebuttals,* 277–295.

C107 "This Must Not Get Out," *Redbook* L (January), 68–73+. Short story.

C108 "English A," *American Mercury* XIII (February), 204–212.

C109 "Father of Waters," *SRL* IV (February 4), 568. Reviews of Harold Speakman, *Mostly Mississippi,* and Lyle Saxon, *Father Mississippi.*

C110 "Mr. Ford's New York," *SRL* IV (February 18), 607. Review of Ford Madox Ford, *New York Is Not America.*

C111 " 'A Chick among You,' " *SRL* IV (March 3), 647. Review of Philip Guedalla, *Conquistador.*

C112 "A Yearbook of Folly," *SRL* IV (March 10), 662. Review of Charles Merz, *The Great American Band Wagon.*

C113 "Image and Symbol," *SRL* IV (April 28), 824–825. Review of Harvey W. Root, *The Unknown Barnum.*

C114 "Jewry in America," *SRL* IV (May 5), 840. Review of Ludwig Lewisohn, *The Island Within.*

C115 "Ranch Wondering," *Post* CC (June 2), 24–25+. Short story.

C116 "Afternoon of a Biologist," *Harper's* CLVII (September), 408–420. Short story.

C117 "Tools for the Intellectual Life," *Harper's* CLVII (October), 602–609.

C118 "Teamwork," *Redbook* LI (October), 66–69+. Short story.

C119 "The Popular Proverbs of Baron O-No," *Post* CCI (October 27), 12–13+. Short story.

C120. "An American Myth," *SRL* V (November 10), 335–336. Review of Richard J. Walsh and Milton S. Salsburg, *The Making of Buffalo Bill.*

C121 "Gaily the Troubador," *Redbook* LII (November), 68–71+. Short story.

C122 "Editions of 'Typee,'" *SRL* V (November 24), 406. Letter to the editor.

C123 "Victoria Woodhull," *SRL* V (December 29), 552. Review of Emanie Sachs, *The Terrible Siren: Victoria Woodhull.*

C124 "The College Angel," *Redbook* LII (December), 72–75+. Short story.

C125 "Exit Robin Hood," *Post* CCI (December 29), 14–15+. Short story.

1929

C126 "A Hymn to America," *SRL* V (January 5), 569. Review of Thomas Williamson, *Stride of Man.*

C127 "The Maddest of All Follies," *Redbook* LII (January), 54–57+. Short story.

C128 "Northwestern," *College Humor* (January), 24–25+. Reprinted as "The Coeds Were Real — The Boys Were Shadows" in *The College Years*, Hawthorn Books, Inc., 1958. (See B29.)

C129 "A History of Revivalism," *SRL* V (April 13), 877. Review of Grover C. Loud, *Evangelized America.*

C130 "Our Local Guelphs," *Post* CCI (April 27), 10–11. Short story.

C131 "Brave Days in Washoe," *American Mercury* XVII (June), 228–237. Reprinted in *Mark Twain's America*, 115–133.

C132 "Frontier America," *SRL* V (June 1), 1067–1068. Review of John P. Fort, *Stone Daugherty*.

C133 "The Penalties of Wisdom," *Redbook* LIII (September), 52–55+. Short story.

1930

*C134 "The Centennial of Mormonism," *American Mercury* XIX (January), 1–13. Reprinted and expanded in *Forays and Rebuttals*, 71–137, and contracted in *The Mormon Century Book*.

C135 "Sea Goddess," *Redbook* LVI (April), 84–87+. Short story.

C136 "The Long Chance," *Post* CCII (April 19), 12–13+. Short story.

C137 "Byron Satterlee Hurlbut," *Harvard* XXXVIII (March), 302–307.

*C138 "The Precarious Attitudes of Robeson Ballou," *Post* CCIII (July 26), 8–9+. Short story.

C139 "From a Graduate's Window," *Harvard* XXXIX (September), 47–50.

C140 "Literary Censorship in Cambridge," *Harvard* XXXIX (September), 30–42.

C141 "The Hand of Fear," *Redbook* LVI (November), 66–69+. Short story.

C142 "Back Bay Nights," *Post* CCIII (November 15), 14–15+. Short story.

C143 "From a Graduate's Window," *Harvard* XXXIX (December), 176–179.

C144 Review of S. E. Morison, *The Development of Harvard University*, *Harvard* XXXIX (December), 260–263.

C145 Review of Robert Hillyer, *The Gates of the Compass*, *Harvard* XXXIX (December), 263–264.

1931

C146 "You Jack o'Diamonds," *Post* CCIII (January 10), 12–13+. Short story.

C147 "From a Graduate's Window," *Harvard* XXXIX (March), 337–348.

C148 "The Frivial Wick," *Post* CCIII (March 28), 8–9+. Short story.

C149 "We Brighter People," *Harvard* XXXIX (March), 323–337. Reprinted as "The Well-informed, 1920–1930" in *Forays and Rebuttals*, 221–239.

C150 "Civilized People," *Redbook* LVII (May), 57–61+. Short story.

C151 "Webersham: The Leland Affair," *Post* CCIII (May 2), 10–11+. Short story.

C152 "From a Graduate's Window," *Harvard* XXXIX (June), 478–494.

C153 "The Real Frontier," subtitle: "A Preface to Mark Twain," *Harper's* CLXIII (June), 60–71. Reprinted with additions in *Mark Twain's America*.

C154 "Summer's End," *Redbook* LVII (September), 57–61+. Short story.

C155 "Prig's Progress," *Post* CCIV (September 12), 10–11+. Short story.

C156 "From a Graduate's Window," *Harvard* XL (September), 84–91.

C157 "The Matrix of Mark Twain's Humour," *The Bookman* LXXIV (October), 172–178. Reprinted with additions in *Mark Twain's America*, 79–99.

C158 "From a Graduate's Window," *Harvard* XL (December), 183–196.

C159 "The Dying Rose," *Post* CCIV (December 5), 12–13+. Short story.

C160 "Mark Twain and the Genteel Tradition," *Harvard* XL (December), 155–163. Reprinted in *Mark Twain's America.*

1932

C161 Review of Clara Clemens, *My Father: Mark Twain, NEQ* V (January), 169–171.

C162 "Accolade," *Post* CCIV (January 16), 6–7+. Short story.

C163 "College Education for the Intelligent Few," *Current History* XXXV (March), 792–798. Original title: "A Dilemma of the Modern College."

C164 "From a Graduate's Window," *Harvard* XL (March), 298–314.

C165 Anonymous, "Grace before Teaching: A Letter to a Young Doctor of Literature," *Harvard* XL (March), 261–275. Reprinted in *Forays and Rebuttals*, 257–276.

C166 "New England: There She Stands," *Harper's* CLXXIV (March), 405–415. Reprinted in *Forays and Rebuttals*, 138–158.

C167 "In Re Mark Twain," *SRL* VIII (April 2), 640. Letter to the editor.

C168 "In Barrasca," [sic] *Post* CCIV (April 23), 8–9+. Short story.

C169 "From a Graduate's Window," *Harvard* XL (June), 408–413.

C170 "Tom, Huck, and America," *SRL* IX (August 13), 37–39. Reprinted in *Mark Twain's America*, 304–308, 314–320.

C171 "The Second Act Curtain," *Post* CCV (September 3), 16–17+. Short story.

1933

C172 "The Skeptical Biographer," *Harper's* CLXVI (January), 181–192. Reprinted in *Forays and Rebuttals*, 179–203.

C173 "Sinclair Lewis," *SRL* IX (January 28), 397–398. Reviews of Sinclair Lewis, *Ann Vickers* and Carl Van Doren, *Sinclair Lewis*. Reprinted as "Ann Vickers by Sinclair Lewis" in *Forays and Rebuttals*, 305–314.

C174 "The Rocking Chair in History and Criticism," *Forum* LXXXIX (February), 104–107.

C175 "American Life," *SRL* IX (March 4), 464. Review of Arthur M. Schlesinger, *The Rise of the City*.

C176 "The Home-Town Mind," *Post* CCV (April 1), 16–17+. Short story.

C177 "Bully Boy," *SRL* IX (April 8), 523. Review of Walter Blair and Franklin J. Meine, *Mink Fink*.

C178 "A Primer for Intellectuals," *SRL* IX (April 22), 545–546.

C179 "DeVoto and Pareto," *SRL* IX (May 20), 607. Letter to the editor.

C180 "Mr. DeVoto Wins," *SRL* X (July 22), 4. Letter to the editor.

C181 "The Girl Who Saved Herself," *Collier's* XCII (August 26), 17+. Short story.

C182 "Jonathan Dyer, Frontiersman," subtitle: "A Paragraph in the History of the West," *Harper's* CLXVII (September), 491–501. Reprinted as "The Life of Jonathan Dyer, Frontiersman" in *Forays and Rebuttals*, 3–24, and in *Rocky Mountain Reader*, New York, Dutton, 1946, 60–76.

C183 "Pareto and Bassett Jones," *SRL* X (September 2), 80. Letter to the editor.

C184 "Sentiment and the Social Order: Introduction to the Teachings of Pareto," *Harper's* CLXVII (October), 569–581.

C185 "Pareto and Fascism," *The New Republic* LXXVI (October 11), 244–245. Letter to the editor.

C186 "The Faculty First," *Harvard* XLII (December), 90–97.

C187 "One Part Cheesecloth," *Post* CCVI (December 9), 16–17+. Short story.

1934

C188 "Champion Preferred," *Collier's* XCIII (January 6), 12+. Short story.

C189 "How Not To Write History," *Harper's* CLXVIII (January), 199–208. Reprinted as "Thinking about America" in *Forays and Rebuttals*, 159–178.

C190 Review of James T. Adams, *Henry Adams*, NEQ VII (March), 195–196.

C191 "Choice of Weapons," *Collier's* XCIII (April 14), 7–9+. Short story.

C192 "Nature's Wise Plan," *Collier's* XCIII (May 5), 25+. Short story.

C193 "Exiles from Reality," *SRL* X (June 2), 721–722. Review of Malcolm Cowley, *Exile's Return*. Reprinted as "Exile's Return" in *Forays and Rebuttals*, 315–323.

C194 "Hail Hale," *SRL* X (June 30), 780. Letter to the editor.

*C195 "The Bulfinch House," by John August, *Harper's* CLXXIX (July), 156–170. Short story.

C196 "Snapshots," by John August, *Harper's* CLXXIX (August), 374–377. (The Lion's Mouth.)

C197 "The West: A Plundered Province," *Harper's* CLXXIX (August), 355–364. Reprinted as "The Plundered Province" in *Forays and Rebuttals*, 46–65.

C198 "The Obvious Thing," *Post* CCVII (September 29), 18–19+. Short story.

C199 "There's Something about a Wedding," *Post* CCVII (October 27), 18–19+. Short story.

C200 Review of Harry Hartwick, *The Foreground of American Fiction*, NEQ VII (December), 741–743.

C201 "Up from the Sextette," *Post* CCVII (December 1), 12–13+. Short story.

C202 "Manhattan Jitters," *Redbook* LXIV (December), 32–35+. Short story.

C203 "The Second Proverb," *Liberty*. Short story.

1935

C204 "The Timid Profession," *Post* CCVII (February 9), 12–13+. Short story.

C205 "She Had To Be Understood," *Collier's* XCV (March 9), 22–23+. Short story.

C206 "Streamline Version of Harold Bell Wright," *SRL* XI (March 30), 581. Review of Lloyd C. Douglas, *Green Light*. Reprinted as "Green Light" in *Forays and Rebuttals*, 345–347.

C207 "Fossil Remnants of the Frontier," subtitle: "Notes on a Utah Boyhood," *Harper's* CLXX (April), 590–600. Reprinted in *Forays and Rebuttals*, 25–45.

C208 "A Novel Hammered Out of Experience," *SRL* XI (April 27), 645+. Review of James Boyd, *Roll River*.

C209 "Trust Company Child," *Collier's* XCV (May 25), 17+. Short story.

C210 "The Importance of Pareto," *SRL* XII (May 25), 11.

C211 "Candlelight in Westover," *Post* CCVIII (July 6), 26+. Short story.

C212 "It's My Town," *Collier's* XCVI (July 27), 10–11+. Short story.

C213 Review of Fred L. Pattee, editor, *Mark Twain Selections*, *NEQ* VIII (September), 427–430.

C214 "View from the Top," *Collier's* XCVI (September 21), 14–15+. Short story.

C215 "Classy Literature," *SRL* XXI (October 5), 26+. Review of Joseph Freeman, editor, *Proletarian Literature in the United States*. Reprinted in *Forays and Rebuttals*, 334–339, in chapter entitled "Proletarian Literature in the United States."

C216 "Hemingway in the Valley," *SRL* XII (October 26), 5. Review of Ernest Hemingway, *Green Hills of Africa*. Reprinted in *Forays and Rebuttals*, 340–344, in chapter entitled "Green Hills of Africa."

C217 "The Greatness of Mark Twain," *NYT Book* (October

27), 1+. Reviews of Albert B. Paine, editor, *Mark Twain's Notebook* and Edward Wagenknecht, *Mark Twain: The Man and His Work.*

C218 "Solidarity at Alexandria," The Easy Chair #1, *Harper's* CLXXI (November), 765–768.

C219 "A Violent, Fighting Pioneer," *SRL* XIII (November 2), 5–6. Review of Mari Sandoz, *Old Jules.* Reprinted in *Forays and Rebuttals,* 66–70.

C220 "The Absolute in the Machine Shop," The Easy Chair #2, *Harper's* CLXXII (December), 125–128. Reprinted in *Forays and Rebuttals,* 213–220.

1936

C221 "Memento for New Year's Day," The Easy Chair #3, *Harper's* CLXXII (January), 253–256.

C222 "Life Begins So Soon," *Collier's* XCVII (February 1), 7–9+; (February 8), 12–13+; (February 15), 16–17+; (February 22), 16–17+; (February 29), 18–19+; (March 7), 14–16+; (March 14), 22+; (March 21), 20–21+; (March 28), 18–19+; (April 4), 20–21+. Fiction. Unpublished in book form. (The DeVoto-Stanford bound copy is entitled "Senior Spring.")

C223 "The Folk Mind," The Easy Chair #4, *Harper's* CLXXII (February), 381–384.

C224 "Terwillinger in Plato's Dream," The Easy Chair #5, *Harper's* CLXXII (March), 493–496.

C225 "The Subject Races," *Cosmopolitan* (April), 52–53+. Short story.

C226 "Another Consociate Family," The Easy Chair #6, *Harper's* CLXXII (April), 605–608. Reprinted in *Forays and Rebuttals,* 296–304.

C227 "Genius Is Not Enough," *SRL* XIII (April 25), 3–4+. Review of Thomas Wolfe, *The Story of a Novel.* Reprinted in *Forays and Rebuttals,* 324–333.

C228 "The Consumer's Automobile," The Easy Chair #7, *Harper's* CLXXII (May), 717–720.

C229 "The Editor-elect," *SRL* XIV (May 30), 9. Announcement of DeVoto's policies.

C230 "What the Next Hour Holds," The Easy Chair #8, *Harper's* CLXXIII (June), 109–112. Reprinted as "What the Next Hour May Bring Forth" in *Forays and Rebuttals*, 204–212.

C231 Review of Edward Wagenknecht, *Mark Twain: The Man and His Work*, *NEQ* IX (June), 332–338.

C232 "Mark Twain and the Limits of Criticism," *Forays and Rebuttals*, 373–403. Paper read before the American Literature Section of the MLA, January 1, 1936.

C233 "On Beginning To Write a Novel," signed "Anonymous," *Harper's* CLXXIII (July), 179–188. (Identified as DeVoto's work in Mattingly, *Bernard DeVoto; A Preliminary Appraisal*.)

C234 "Notes on the Red Parnassus," The Easy Chair #9, *Harper's* CLXXIII (July), 221–224.

C235 "How To Live among the Vermonters," The Easy Chair #10, *Harper's* CLXXIII (August), 333–336.

C236 "John Dos Passos: Anatomist of Our Time," *SRL* XIV (August 8), 3–4+. Review of *The Big Money* and other works.

C237 Review of Walter and Margaret Hard, *This Is Vermont*, *SRL* XIV (August 22), 23.

C238 "A Puritan Tercentenary," The Easy Chair #11, *Harper's* CLXXIII (September), 445–448.

C239 "A Generation beside the Limpopo," *SRL* XIV (September 26), 3–4+. Reprinted in *Minority Report*, 139–150.

C240 "Prize Novels," *SRL* XIV (September 26), 8. Editorial.

C241 "Reviewing Reviews," *SRL* XIV (September 26), 26–27.

C242 "One Man's Guess," The Easy Chair #12, *Harper's* CLXXIII (October), 557–560.

C243 "Civilization in the U.S.A.," *SRL* XIV (October 3), 7. Review of Gilbert Seldes, *Mainland*.

C244 "The 42nd Parallel," *SRL* XIV (October 3), 8. Editorial.

C245 "The Code Napoleon," *SRL* XIV (October 10), 10. Editorial.

C246 "Crackerbox Commentator," *SRL* XIV (October 10), 5. Review of Westbrook Pegler, *'Taint Right.*

C247 Review of Idwal Jones, *China Boy*, *SRL* XIV (October 10), 35.

C248 "Reviewing Reviews," *SRL* XIV (October 10), 37.

C249 "Horizon Land (1)," *SRL* XIV (October 17), 8. Editorial. Reprinted in *Minority Report*, 284–287, in chapter entitled "Costume Piece."

C250 "Beyond Studs Lonigan," *SRL* XIV (October 24), 5–6. Review of James T. Farrell, *A World I Never Made.*

C251 "Eppur Si Muove," *SRL* XIV (October 24), 8. Editorial. Reprinted in *Minority Report*, 339–343, in chapter entitled "Overlooking the Campus." (Printed as "Eppur Si Move.")

C252 "Mirrors of Forty-fifth Street," *SRL* XIV (October 24), 6.

C253 Review of T. J. Maloney, editor, *U.S. Camera, 1936*, *SRL* XV (October 31), 20.

C254 "Unemployed Writers," *SRL* XV (October 31), 8. Editorial.

C255 "Witchcraft in Mississippi," *SRL* XV (October 31), 3–4+. Review of William Faulkner, *Absalom, Absalom!* Reprinted in *Minority Report*, 209–218.

C256 "On Moving to New York," The Easy Chair #13, *Harper's* CLXXIII (November), 669–672. Reprinted in *Minority Report*, 40–47.

C257 "Stercoraceous Comment," *SRL* XV (November 7), 8. Editorial. Reprinted in *Minority Report*, 332–336, in chapter entitled, "Overlooking the Campus."

C258 "Delphic Apollo in Illinois," *SRL* XV (November 14), 5. Review of Edgar Lee Masters, *Across Spoon River.*

C259 "Realism for Children," *SRL* XV (November 14), 8. Editorial.

C260 "Political Coda," *SRL* XV (November 14), 8. Editorial.

C261 "Minority Report," *SRL* XV (November 21), 3–4+.
Reprinted as "Monte Cristo in Modern Dress" in
Minority Report, 190–197.

C262 "The Reference Shelf," *SRL* XV (November 21), 8.
Editorial.

C263 "Regionalism or the Coterie Manifesto," *SRL* XV (November 28), 8. Editorial.

C264 "Seed Corn and Mistletoe," The Easy Chair #14, *Harper's*
CLXXIV (December), 109–112. Reprinted in *Minority Report*, 32–39.

C265 "Passage to India," *SRL* XV (December 5), 3–4+. Reprinted in *Minority Report*, 3–15.

C266 "Reviewing Reviews," *SRL* XV (December 5), 58–59.

C267 "Sir:" *SRL* XV (December 12), 8. Editorial. Reprinted
in *Minority Report*, 298–300, in chapter entitled "On
Notions."

C268 "Vardis Fisher in Salt Lake City," *SRL* XV (December
12), 8. Editorial.

C269 "Reading for Pleasure," *SRL* XV (December 19), 8. Editorial.

C270 "The American Scholar," *SRL* XV (December 26), 9+.
Editorial. Reprinted in *Minority Report*, 343–346, in
chapter entitled "Overlooking the Campus."

1937

C271 "Tyranny at Longfellow School," The Easy Chair #15,
Harper's CLXXIV (January), 221–224.

C272 "The Brahmin Way of Life," *SRL* XV (January 2), 5.
Review of John P. Marquand, *The Late George Apley*.

C273 "A Hard Life," *SRL* XV (January 2), 8. Editorial.

C274 "Gargantua in Modern Dress," *SRL* XV (January 9), 15.
Review of François Rabelais translated by Jacques Le
Clercy, *Gargantua and Pantagruel*.

C275 "How To Be a Publisher (1)," *SRL* XV (January 9), 8.
Editorial.

C276 "The Library Crisis," *SRL* XV (January 16), 8. Editorial.

C277 "Reviewing Reviews," *SRL* XV (January 16), 19–20.

C278 "Reviewing Reviews," *SRL* XV (January 30), 8. Editorial.

C279 "The Test of Time," *SRL* XV (January 30), 14. Review of W. Somerset Maugham, *The Moon and Sixpence,* 1919.

C280 "The Future of the Longfellow School," The Easy Chair #16, *Harper's* CLXXIV (February), 333–336.

C281 "The Specialist," *SRL* XV (February 6), 8. Editorial. Reprinted in *Minority Report,* 304–308, in chapter entitled "On Notions."

C282 "My Dear Edmund Wilson," *SRL* XV (February 13), 8+. Editorial. Expanded as "Autobiography: or, As Some Call It, Literary Criticism," in *Minority Report,* 163–189.

C283 "About-face of Mr. Stearns," *SRL* XV (February 20), 8. Editorial. Reprinted in *Minority Report,* 328–331, in chapter entitled "Back Eddies."

C284 "Magistrate Curran's Opinion," *SRL* XV (February 20), 8. Editorial.

C285 "The First WPA Guide," *SRL* XV (February 27), 8. Editorial.

C286 "Distempers of the Press," The Easy Chair #17, *Harper's* CLXXIV (March), 445–448. Reprinted in *Minority Report,* 56–63.

C287 "The Bonnie Blue Flag," *SRL* XV (March 6), 8. Editorial. Reprinted in *Minority Report,* 281–284, in chapter entitled "Costume Piece."

C288 "Don't Miss Old Faithful," *SRL* XV (March 6), 8. Editorial.

C289 "Master of Two Dimensions," *SRL* XV (March 6), 3. Review of W. Somerset Maugham, *Theatre.*

C290 "Reviewing Reviews," *SRL* XV (March 6), 25.

C291 "The Pulitzer Prize in History," *SRL* XV (March 13), 3–4+.

C292 "William Dean Howells," *SRL* XV (March 13), 8. Editorial.

C293 "Amateur History," *SRL* XV (March 20), 8. Editorial.

C294 "The Chosen People," *SRL* XV (March 20), 5–6. Review of Pierrepont B. Noyes, *My Father's House.*

C295 "Agitated Ladies," *SRL* XV (March 27), 8. Editorial.

C296 "Author and Publisher," *SRL* XV (March 27), 3A–4A+.

C297 "Perils of Pauline," *SRL* XV (March 27), 8. Editorial. Reprinted in *Minority Report,* 312, in chapter entitled "On Notions."

C298 "Soliloquy in Arizona," *SRL* XV (March 27), 5. Review of J. B. Priestley, *Midwest on the Desert: Excursion into Autobiography.*

C299 "Not a Personal Essay," The Easy Chair #18, *Harper's* CLXXIV (April), 557–560.

C300 "At the Cannon's Mouth," *SRL* XV (April 3), 8. Editorial. Reprinted in *Minority Report,* 317–320, in chapter entitled "Back Eddies."

C301 "In Pursuit of an Idea," *SRL* XV (April 3), 6–7. Review of Josephine Johnson, *Jordanstown.*

C302 "Reviewing Reviews," *SRL* XV (April 3), 32+.

C303 "Enlightened Research," *SRL* XV (April 10), 8. Editorial.

C304 "Reviewing Reviews," *SRL* XV (April 17), 8.

C305 "The Modern Keyhole," *SRL* XV (April 17), 8. Editorial. Reprinted in *Minority Report,* 313–317, in chapter entitled "Back Eddies."

C306 "Horizon Land (2)," *SRL* XV (April 24), 8. Editorial. Reprinted as "Continental Divide" in *Minority Report,* 287–291.

C307 " 'Liberal' Equals Nnx," The Easy Chair #19, *Harper's* CLXXIV (May), 669–672. Reprinted in *Minority Report,* 104–111.

C308 "Germany in the Vortex," *SRL* XVI (May 1), 3–4. Review of Erich Maria Remarque, *Three Comrades.*

C309 "Nymph," *SRL* XVI (May 8), 8. Editorial. Reprinted

in *Minority Report,* 292–296, in chapter entitled "On Notions."

C310 "The Pulitzer Prize Winners," *SRL* XVI (May 8), 3–4.

C311 "Proposal to Contributors, Proposal to Publishers, Proposal to a Pulitzer Committee," *SRL* XVI (May 15), 9. Editorial.

C312 Review of James T. Farrell, *Can All This Grandeur Perish? SRL* XVI (May 22), 20–21.

C313 "The Writer's Congress," *SRL* XVI (May 22), 8. Editorial. Reprinted in *Minority Report,* 273–276, in chapter entitled "Crackle on the Left."

C314 "Always Different, Always the Same," *SRL* XVI (May 29), 3–4+. Reviews of Burton Rascoe, *Before I Forget* and Malcolm Cowley, editor, *After the Genteel Tradition.* Reprinted as "Plus Ce Change" in *Minority Report,* 151–162.

C315 "Reviewing Reviews," *SRL* XVI (May 29), 21–22.

C316 "The Frustrate Censor," The Easy Chair #20, *Harper's* CLXXV (June), 109–112.

C317 "Invitation to the Waltz," *SRL* XVI (June 5), 8. Editorial. Reprinted in *Minority Report,* 277–280, in chapter entitled "Crackle on the Left."

C318 "Rhapsody in Green," *SRL* XVI (June 5), 11–12. Reviews of Charles Edward Crane, *Let Me Show You Vermont;* Frederick F. Van de Water, *A Home in the Country;* and Vrest Orton Weston, *And So Goes Vermont.*

*C319 "A Date for Thursday," by John August, *Collier's,* XLIX (June 12), 48+. Short story. Original title, "An Hour on Sunday."

C320 "Opportunities," *SRL* XVI (June 19), 8. Editorial.

C321 "Reviewing Reviews," *SRL* XVI (June 19), 21–22.

C322 "English '37," *SRL* XVI (June 26), 8–9; (July 3), 8–9; (July 10), 8+; (July 17), 8+; (July 24), 8+; (July 31), 8+; (August 7), 8+; (August 14), 8+; (August 21), 8+; (August 28), 8+; (September 4), 8+. Subtitled "The Novelist and the Reader." This material is used as the basis of chapters VII through XI in *The World of Fiction*. Each installment printed on editorial page.

C323 "The Cestus of Hygiea," The Easy Chair #21, *Harper's* CLXXV (July), 221–224.

C324 Review of Kenneth Roberts, *Northwest Passage*, SRL XVI (July 3), 5.

C325 "Reviewing Reviews," *SRL* (July 17), 20.

C326 "Gettysburg," The Easy Chair #22, *Harper's* CLXXV (August), 333–336. Reprinted in *Minority Report*, 16–23.

C327 "Reviewing Reviews," *SRL* XVI (August 14), 16.

C328 "Page from a Primer," The Easy Chair #23, *Harper's* CLXXV (September), 445–448. Reprinted in *Minority Report*, 24–31.

C329 "Reviewing Reviews," *SRL* XVI (September 18), 22.

C330 "The Lineage of Eustace Tilley," *SRL* XVI (September 25), 3–4+. Review of Walter Blair, editor, *Native American Humor 1800–1900*.

C331 "What of the Night?" *SRL* XVI (September 25), 8. Editorial. Reprinted in *Minority Report*, 296–298, in chapter entitled "On Notions."

C332 "The WPA Guides," *SRL* XVI (September 25), 8. Editorial.

C333 "Desertion from the New Deal," The Easy Chair #24, *Harper's* CLXXV (October), 557–560.

C334 "A Sagebrush Bookshelf," *Harper's* CLXXV (October), 488–496.

C335 "Death of the Sentence," *SRL* XVI (October 2), 8. Editorial. Reprinted in *Minority Report*, 265–269, in chapter entitled "Rule or Ruin."

C336 "Grammarian's Funeral," *SRL* XVI (October 9), 9. Editorial. Reprinted in *Minority Report*, 269–272, in chapter entitled "Rule or Ruin."

C337 "Reviewing Reviews," *SRL* XVI (October 9), 38–39.

C338 "Writing for Money," *SRL* XVI (October 9), 3–4+. Reprinted in *Minority Report*, 244–253.

C339 "Tiger, Tiger!" *SRL* XVI (October 16), 8. Editorial. Reprinted in *Minority Report*, 257–261, in chapter entitled "Lycanthropy."

C340 "Rats, Lice, and Poetry," *SRL* XVI (October 23), 8. Editorial. Reprinted in *Minority Report*, 261–264, in chapter entitled "Lycanthropy."

C341 "The Logic of Sentiment," *SRL* XVII (October 30), 8. Editorial. Reprinted in *Minority Report*, 301–304, in chapter entitled "On Notions."

C342 "The Liberation of Spring City," The Easy Chair #25, *Harper's* CLXXV (November), 669–672. Reprinted in *Minority Report*, 64–71.

C343 "Writing American History," *SRL* XVII (November 6), 8. Editorial.

C344 "Books and Cameras," *SRL* XVII (November 6), 8. Editorial.

C345 "Pseudo," *SRL* XVII (November 6), 8. Editorial.

C346 "Dictionaries for Children," *SRL* XVII (November 13), 8. Editorial.

C347 "Mene, Mene," *SRL* XVII (November 20), 8. Editorial.

C348 "Our Dried Voices," *SRL* XVII (November 27), 8. Editorial. Reprinted in *Minority Report*, 321–324, in chapter entitled "Back Eddies."

C349 "Five-Cent Christmas Card," The Easy Chair #26, *Harper's* CLXXVI (December), 109–112.

C350 "Christmas Tonic," *SRL* XVII (December 4), 12. Editorial.

C351 "Reviewing Reviews," *SRL* XVII (December 4), 52.

C352 "The Faculty Style," *SRL* XVII (December 18), 8. Editorial. Reprinted in *Minority Report*, 336–339, in chapter entitled "Overlooking the Campus."

C353 "Fiction Fights the Civil War," *SRL* XVII (December 18), 3–4+.

C354 "Great Circle," *SRL* XVII (December 25), 8. Editorial.

Reprinted in *Minority Report*, 308–312, in chapter entitled "On Notions."

1938

C355 "Good and Wicked Words," The Easy Chair #27, *Harper's* CLXXVI (January), 221–224. Reprinted in *Minority Report*, 120–127.

C356 "Ace in the Hole," *SRL* XVII (January 1), 8. Editorial.

C357 "The Critics and Robert Frost," *SRL* XVII (January 1), 3–4+. Review of Richard Thornton, editor, *Recognition of Robert Frost*.

C358 "Shallow Waters," *SRL* XVII (January 8), 8. Editorial.

C359 "Report on Photography," *SRL* XVII (January 15), 8. Editorial.

C360 "The Test of Time," *SRL* XVII (January 22), 8. Editorial. Reprinted in *Minority Report*, 325–328, in chapter entitled "Back Eddies."

C361 "C-Plus Fiction," *SRL* XVII (January 29), 8. Editorial.

C362 "Friday Afternoon at Country Day," The Easy Chair #28, *Harper's* CLXXVI (February), 333–336. Reprinted in *Minority Report*, 235–243.

C363 "The Second Step," *SRL* XVII (February 5), 8. Editorial.

C364 "Romans à Clef," *SRL* XVII (February 12), 8; (February 19), 8; (March 5), 8. Printed on editorial page.

C365 "Faulkner's South," *SRL* XVII (February 19), 5. Review of William Faulkner, *The Unvanquished*.

C366 "Fiction Drowned in Talk," *SRL* XVII (February 26), 19. Review of Aline Bernstein, *The Journey Down*.

C367 "Those Who Can Write," *SRL* XVII (February 26), 8. Editorial.

C368 "The Game and the Candle," The Easy Chair #29, *Harper's* CLXXVI (March), 445–448.

C369 "Mark Twain: A Caricature," *SRL* XVII (March 19), 5. Review of Edgar Lee Masters, *Mark Twain: A Portrait*.

C370 "U.S. One," *SRL* XVII (March 19), 8. Editorial.

*C371 "A Demurrer," *The Middlebury College News Letter*, (March 1938), 15–16, 19. Speech in acceptance of Honorary Litt. D., 1937. (See D4.)

C372 "Notes on a Centennial," The Easy Chair #30, *Harper's* CLXXVI (April), 557–560.

C373 "Reminiscence," *SRL* XVII (April 2), 12. Editorial.

C374 "The River," *SRL* XVII (April 9), 8. Editorial.

C375 "Sweet English," *SRL* XVII (April 9), 9. Letter to the editor.

C376 "Notes on the American Way," The Easy Chair #31, *Harper's* CLXXVI (May), 669–672.

C377 "New England Via W.P.A.," *SRL* XVII (May 14), 3–4+.

*C378 "The Fallacy of Excess Interpretation," The Easy Chair #32, *Harper's* CLXXVII (June), 109–112. Reprinted in *Minority Report*, 112–119.

C379 "Fiction and the Everlasting If," *Harper's* CLXXVII (June), 42–49. Subtitled: "Notes on the Contemporary Historical Novel."

C380 "The Day We Celebrate," The Easy Chair #33, *Harper's* CLXXVII (July), 221–224.

C381 "On Moving from New York," The Easy Chair #34, *Harper's* CLXXVII (August), 333–336. Reprinted in *Reader's Digest* (November), 108. Reprinted in *Minority Report*, 48–55.

C382 "Letters from America," The Easy Chair #35, *Harper's* CLXXVII (September), 445–448.

C383 "Vacation," The Easy Chair #36, *Harper's* CLXXVII (October), 557–560.

C384 "DeVoto To Edit Mark Twain Papers," *SRL* XVIII (October 15), 13. Letter to the editor.

C385 "Snow White and the Seven Dreads," The Easy Chair #37, *Harper's* CLXXVII (November), 669–672. Reprinted in *Minority Report*, 219–226.

C386 "Paradox on Betelgeuse," The Easy Chair #38, *Harper's* CLXXVIII (December), 109–112. Reprinted in *Minority Report*, 88–95.

C387 "The Mark Twain Papers," *SRL* XIX (December 10), 3–4+.

C388 "Mark Twain Papers," *SRL* XIX (December 10), 9. Letter to the editor.

1939

C389 "From Dream to Fiction," The Easy Chair #39, *Harper's* CLXXVIII (January), 221–224. Reprinted in *Minority Report*, 227–234 and *The World of Fiction*, 25–44.

C390 "Hoop Skirts and Buena Vista," The Easy Chair #40, *Harper's* CLXXVIII (February), 333–336.

C391 "Wisdom Lingers," The Easy Chair #41, *Harper's* CLXXVIII (March), 445–448. Reprinted in *Minority Report*, 96–103.

C392 Review of Cyril Clemens, *My Cousin Mark Twain*, *SRL* XIX (March 11), 16.

*C393 "Home Thoughts from Vermont," the *Pan* I (March). (The *Pan* was published in protest to the censorship of the *Pen* by University of Utah authorities. It was published off-campus and issued from a café near campus.)

C394 Review of James Boyd, *Bitter Creek*, *SRL* XIX (March 18), 6.

C395 "The Paring Knife at the Crossroads," The Easy Chair #42, *Harper's* CLXXVIII (April), 557–560.

C396 "G. and S. Preferred," The Easy Chair #43, *Harper's* CLXXVIII (May), 669–672.

C397 "Mark Twain about the Jews," *Jewish Frontier* (May). Reprinted in *Jewish Frontier Anthology*, 1934–1944 (New York: Jewish Frontier Association), 1945, 177–181. (See B19.)

C398 "What's the Matter with History?" The Easy Chair #44, *Harper's* CLXXIX (June), 109–112.

C399 Review of Thomas D. Clark, *The Rampaging Frontier*, *NYT Book* (June 25), 5.

C400 "Aftermath of a Cocktail Party," *New Republic* LXXXXIX (June 28), 218. Letter to the editor.

C401 "Unrest in the Kitchen," The Easy Chair #45, *Harper's* CLXXIX (July), 221–224.

C402 "Thou and the Camel," *Cosmopolitan* (July), 58–61+. Short story.

C403 "The Terror," The Easy Chair #46, *Harper's* CLXXIX (August), 333–336. Reprinted in *Minority Report*, 72–79.

C404 "Millennial Millions," *SRL* XX (August 26), 3–4+. Review of Vardis Fisher, *Children of God*.

C405 "Doom Beyond Jupiter," The Easy Chair #47, *Harper's* CLXXIX (September), 445–448.

C406 "Meditation in Fading Sunlight," The Easy Chair #48, *Harper's* CLXXIX (October), 557–560. Reprinted in *Minority Report*, 80–87.

C407 "Freud's Influence on Literature," *SRL* XX (October 7), 10–11.

C408 "The Sound of Silk," by John August, *Collier's* CIV (October 21), 9–10+. Short story.

C409 "The Oncoming," The Easy Chair #49, *Harper's* CLXXIX (November), 669–672. Reprinted in *Minority Report*, 128–135.

C410 "Widower's House," *SRL* XXI (November 4), 10–12. Review of Havelock Ellis, *My Life*, reprinted in *Minority Report*, 198–208.

C411 "Luke II, 1," The Easy Chair #50, *Harper's* CLXXX (December), 109–112.

1940

*C412 "American Novels: 1939," *Atlantic* CLXV (January), 66–74.

C413 "The Threshold of Fiction," The Easy Chair #51, *Harper's* CLXXX (January), 221–224. Used in *The World of Fiction*.

C414 "Father Abraham," The Easy Chair #52, *Harper's* CLXXX (February), 333–336.

C415 "Anabasis in Buckskin," *Harper's* CLXXX (March), 400–410.

*C416 "The Engulfed Cathedral," The Easy Chair #53, *Harper's* CLXXX (March), 445–448.

C417 "Freud in American Literature," *Psychoanalytic Quarterly* IX (April), 236–245.

*C418 "Maternity Floor," The Easy Chair #54, *Harper's* CLXXX (April), 557–560. Reprinted in *Reader's Digest* (May 1940), 101–104.

C419 "Remember the Pink Lady?" The Easy Chair #55, *Harper's* CLXXX (May), 669–672.

C420 "Ninetieth Anniversary," The Easy Chair #56, *Harper's* CLXXXI (June), 109–112.

C421 "Position Maintained," The Easy Chair #57, *Harper's* CLXXXI (July), 221–224. Reprinted as "Preface Continued" in *Minority Report*, 221–224.

C422 "Letter from Santa Fe," The Easy Chair #58, *Harper's* CLXXXI (August), 333–336.

C423 "Notes from a Wayside Inn," The Easy Chair #59, *Harper's* CLXXXI (September), 445–448.

C424 "Road Test," The Easy Chair #60, *Harper's* CLXXXI (October), 557–560.

C425 "All Quiet along the Huron," The Easy Chair #61, *Harper's* CLXXXI (November), 669–672.

C426 "Main Street Twenty Years After," *Harper's* CLXXXI (November), 580–587. Reprinted in *Reader's Digest* (December), 1–5.

C427 "To Our New Prophets," The Easy Chair #62, *Harper's* CLXXXI (December), 109–112.

C428 Review of Franklin Walker and G. Ezra Dane, editors, *Mark Twain Travels with Mr. Brown, NYHT Book* XVII (December 29).

1941

C429 "The Mugwump on November 6th," The Easy Chair #63, *Harper's* CLXXXII (January), 221–224.

C430 "Holidays, 1940," The Easy Chair #64, *Harper's* CLXXXII (February), 333–336.

C431 "Easy Steps for Little Feet," The Easy Chair #65, *Harper's* CLXXXII (March), 445–448.

C432 "Manifest Destiny," The Easy Chair #66, *Harper's* CLXXXII (April), 557–560.

C433 "Mark Twain vs. Winston Churchill," *Reader's Digest* (April), 110. Reprinted from *Mark Twain in Eruption*.

*C434 "What to Tell the Young," The Easy Chair #67, *Harper's* CLXXXII (May), 669–672.

C435 Review of Clifford Dowdey, *Sing for a Penny, NYHT Book* XVII (May 11), 4.

C436 "For the Boys of '41," *W Day* (June), 10–11+.

C437 "Stephen Foster's Songs," The Easy Chair #68, *Harper's* CLXXXIII (June), 109–112. (Revised and included in *The Year of Decision*, 133–135.)

C438 "The Image of Napoleon," The Easy Chair #69, *Harper's* CLXXXIII (July), 221–224.

*C439 "Touring New England," *Harper's* CLXXXIII (July), 129–138.

*C440 "Either — Or," The Easy Chair #70, *Harper's* CLXXXIII (August), 333–336.

*C441 Review of Thomas Beer, *Hanna, Crane,* and *The Mauve Decade, NYHT Book* XVII (August 24), 6.

C442 "Under Which King, Bezonian?" The Easy Chair #71, *Harper's* CLXXXIII (September), 445–448.

C443 "Information Please," *SRL* XXIV (September 27), 9. Letter to the editor.

C444 "Portico with Images," The Easy Chair #72, *Harper's* CLXXXIII (October), 557–560.

C445 "Report on the Summer Quarter," The Easy Chair #73, *Harper's* CLXXXIII (November), 669–672.

C446 "Lee Foster Hartman," The Easy Chair #74, *Harper's* CLXXXIV (December), 109–112. Reprinted in memorial volume: *Lee Foster Hartman, Editor of Harper's Magazine, 1931–1941, Harper's*, 1941. (See B14.)

1942

C447 "The Writer's Project," The Easy Chair #75, *Harper's* CLXXXIV (January), 221–224.

C448 "The Lord Helps Those . . .," *Reader's Digest* (January), 21. Reprinted from *Mark Twain in Eruption.*

*C449 "Lecture to a Woman's Club," The Easy Chair #76, *Harper's* CLXXXIV (February), 333–336.

C450 "The Civilian Outpost," The Easy Chair #77, *Harper's* CLXXXIV (March), 445–448.

C451 "Toward Chancellorsville," The Easy Chair #78, *Harper's* CLXXXIV (April), 557–560.

C452 "Lincoln to the 164th Ohio," The Easy Chair #79, *Harper's* CLXXXIV (May), 669–672.

C453 "Sedition's General Staff," The Easy Chair #80, *Harper's* CLXXXV (June), 109–112.

C454 "B. DeV. Also," *SRL* XXV (June 13). Letter to the editor.

*C455 "Commencement Address," The Easy Chair #81, *Harper's* CLXXXV (July), 221–224.

C456 "The Year of Decision." *Atlantic* CLXX (July), 77–84; (August), 79–94; (September), 111–126; (October), 113–125; (November), 109–125. (See A12.)

C457 "Give It to Us Straight," The Easy Chair #82, *Harper's* CLXXXV (August), 333–336.

C458 "Triangular Bandages Go on Babies," The Easy Chair #83, *Harper's* CLXXXV (September), 445–448.

C459 Review of Richard G. Lillard, *Desert Challenge, NYHT Book* XIX (September 20), 3.

*C460 "Dead Center," The Easy Chair #84, *Harper's* CLXXXV (October), 557–560.

*C461 "The Confederate Military System," *SRL* XXV (October 24), 15. Review of Douglas Southall Freeman, *Lee's Lieutenants*, vol. I.

C462 "Wanted: More News!" The Easy Chair #85, *Harper's* CLXXXV (November), 669–672.

C463 "Wait a Minute, Dorothy," The Easy Chair #86, *Harper's* CLXXXVI (December), 109–112.

*C464 "War Is the Life I Live," *W Day* (December), 12–13+.

1943

C465 The Easy Chair #87, *Harper's* CLXXXVI (January), 221–224. Entitled in DeVoto's hand in his bound copy "A Psychiatrist on War."

(The next eighty "Easy Chairs" rarely have titles. When DeVoto has titled them in his own copy, we have so noted. At times *Harper's Magazine* supplied titles on the cover or in the index; these Robert Edson Lee used in his dissertation and they have been noted to facilitate reference.)

C466 "Parkman's Early Diaries," *SRL* XXVI (January 16), 11. Letter to the editor.

C467 The Easy Chair #88, *Harper's* CLXXXVI (February), 333–336. Entitled in DeVoto's hand in his bound copy "To Be Filed, Probably."

C468 The Easy Chair #89, *Harper's* CLXXXVI (March), 437–440. Entitled in DeVoto's hand in his copy "Writers and the War."

C469 "The End in View," *W Day* (March).

C470 "An Exciting Batch of Assorted Prejudices," *NYHT Book*, XIX (March 14), 4. Review of Rose Wilder Lane, *The Discovery of Freedom*.

C471 The Easy Chair #90, *Harper's* CLXXXVI (April), 541–544. Entitled in DeVoto's hand in his copy, "The Worst Mistake."

C472 The Easy Chair #91, *Harper's* CLXXXVI (May), 645–

648. Entitled in DeVoto's hand in his own copy, "Distress under the Elms."

*C473 "Mr. Freeman's Continuing Study," *SRL* XXVI (May 29), 16. Review of Douglas Southall Freeman, *Lee's Lieutenants*, vol. II.

*C474 The Easy Chair #92, *Harper's* CLXXXVII (June), 93–96. Identified on *Harper's* cover as "The Egypt of the West."

*C475 "Seed Time of the New World," *NYT Book* (June 27), 1+. Review of Stephen Vincent Benet, *Western Star*.

C476 The Easy Chair #93, *Harper's* CLXXXVII (July), 129–132.

C477 The Easy Chair #94, *Harper's* CLXXXVII (August), 236–239.

C478 The Easy Chair #95, *Harper's* CLXXXVII (September), 338–341.

C479 The Easy Chair #96, *Harper's* CLXXXVII (October), 435–438.

C480 "A Natural History of Politics," *NYHT Book* XX (October 17), 4. Review of Wilfred E. Binkley, *American Political Parties*.

C481 The Easy Chair #97, *Harper's* CLXXXVII (November), 525–528.

C482 "Go Ahead and Holler," *Reader's Digest* (November), 34.

*C483 The Easy Chair #98, *Harper's* CLXXXVIII (December), 36–39.

1944

C484 The Easy Chair #99, Harper's CLXXXVIII (January), 141–144. Identified in *Harper's* index as "Mr. and Mrs. Charles A. Lindbergh."

C485 The Easy Chair #100, Harper's CLXXXVIII (February), 242–245. Entitled in Lee as "Review of New Books."

C486 The Easy Chair #101, Harper's CLXXXVIII (March), 344–347. Entitled in Lee as "Fear of the Coming Peace."

*C487 "Geopolitics with the Dew on It," *Harper's* CLXXXVIII (March), 313–323.

*C488 The Easy Chair #102, *Harper's* CLXXXVIII (April), 426–429. Entitled in Lee as "Lost Generation of World War II."

C489 "They Turned Their Backs on America," *SRL* XXVII (April 8), 5–8. Reprinted in *The Literary Fallacy* as part of the concluding chapter, and in the *Saturday Review Treasury* under the title "The Great Feud" 265–272. New York, Simon and Schuster, 1957.

C490 "First of the Great Lakes To Be 'Discovered,'" *NYHT Book* XX (April 9), 3. Review of Fred Landon, *Lake Huron*.

*C491 The Easy Chair #103, *Harper's* CLXXXVIII (May), 525–528. Entitled in Lee as "Boston Mobs *Strange Fruit*."

C492 "Older Than God," *W Day* (June). Reprinted in the *Chicago Daily News* (July 12).

C493 The Easy Chair #104, *Harper's* CLXXXIX (June), 44–47. Entitled in Lee as "Willkie, Dewey and the G.O.P."

C494 The Easy Chair #105, *Harper's* CLXXXIX (July), 148–151. Entitled in Lee as "Censorship in Boston."

C495 The Easy Chair #106, *Harper's* CLXXXIX (August), 237–240. Entitled in Lee as "Religious Intolerance."

C496 "The Maturity of American Literature," *SRL* XXVII (August 5), 14–18.

C497 The Easy Chair #107, *Harper's* CLXXXIX (September), 330–333. Entitled in Lee as "Hatch-Connally 'Clean Vote' Bill."

C498 "On 'The Road Back' Following Three Wars," *NYHT Book* XXI (September 17), 1+. Review of Dixon Wecter, *When Johnnie Comes Marching Home*.

C499 "The Falsity of Geopolitics in an Air Age," *NYHT Book* XXI (September 24), 1. Review of Hans W. Weigert and Vilhjalmur Stefansson, editors, *Compass of the World*.

C500 "Let's Not Play College Again," *W Day* (October), 28–29+.

C501 The Easy Chair #108, *Harper's* CLXXXIX (October), 426–429. Entitled in Lee as "Nationalism."

C502 "Short Course in American History," *Good Housekeeping* CXIX (October), 25+.

*C503 The Easy Chair #109, *Harper's* CLXXXIX (November), 554–557. Entitled in Lee as "The South."

C504 The Easy Chair #110, *Harper's* CXC (December), 34–37.

1945

C505 The Easy Chair #111, *Harper's* CXC (January), 133–136. Entitled in Lee as "Thomas E. Dewey."

C506 "How Do *You* Feel about Compulsory Military Training?" *W Day* (February), 28+.

C507 The Easy Chair #112, *Harper's* CXC (February), 225–228. Entitled in Lee as "Literary Censorship."

C508 The Easy Chair #113, *Harper's* CXC (March), 311–314. Entitled in Lee as "The Lewis and Clark Expedition."

C509 The Easy Chair #114, *Harper's* CXC (April), 410–413. Entitled in Lee as "Conscription."

*C510 The Easy Chair #115, *Harper's* CXC (May), 500–503. Entitled in Lee as "Diary of a Public Man."

*C511 The Easy Chair #116, *Harper's* CXC (June), 602–605. Entitled in Lee as "Emily Dickinson."

C512 "Mr. DeVoto Explains As to Use of the Name, Mark Twain," *The Twainian*, vol. 4, no. 9 (June), 2. Letter to the editor.

*C513 The Easy Chair #117, *Harper's* CXCI (July), 33–36. Entitled in Lee as "Norman Corwin." Reprinted as "On a Note of Triumph" in *The Easy Chair*, 127–134.

C514 "Well, How Neurotic Are You?" *W Day* (July), 26–27+.

*C515 The Easy Chair #118, *Harper's* CXCI (August), 134–137. Entitled in Lee as "University of Texas."

C516 "The Great Story of Plymouth Plantation," *NYHT Book* XXI (August 5), 1+. Review of George F. Willison, *Saints and Strangers*.

C517 "Yarbs and Doctor Stuff," *NYHT Book* XXI (August 12), 6. Review of Madge E. Pickard and R. Carlyle Buley, *The Mid-west Pioneer.*

*C518 The Easy Chair #119, *Harper's* CXCI (September), 222–225. Entitled in Lee as "State of the Union."

*C519 "When Social History Becomes Literature," *NYHT Book* XXII (September 16), 1+. Review of Arthur M. Schlesinger, Jr., *The Age of Jackson.*

*C520 The Easy Chair #120, *Harper's* CXCI (October), 325–328. Entitled in Lee as "V-J Day."

C521 "America's West and Mid-West in Literature," *NYHT Book* XXII (October 14), 1. Reviews of three anthologies.

C522 "The Rare Exciting Exercise of Thinking," *NYHT Book* XXII (October 21), 5. Review of Charles P. Curtis, Jr., and Ferris Greenslet, editors, *The Practical Cogitator.*

C523 Review of *The Wild Horse of the West* by Walker D. Wyman, *American Historical Review* LI (October), 174–175.

C524 "Barker up the Wrong Tree?" *Harper's* CXCI (November), unpaged. In the "Personal & Otherwise" column.

*C525 The Easy Chair #121, *Harper's* CXCI (November), 410–413.

C526 "A Reactionary Decision," *Author's League Bulletin* XXXIII (November), 9–10.

C527 "A Revaluation," *Rocky Mountain Review* X (Autumn), 7–11.

C528 The Easy Chair #122, *Harper's* CXCI (December), 505–508.

C529 "The Case of the Prophet, Joseph Smith," *NYHT Book* XXII (December 16), 1. Review of Fawn M. Brodie, *No Man Knows My History. The Life of Joseph Smith.*

1946

C530 "The Flapper's Revolution," *W Day* (January), 26–27+.

C531 The Easy Chair #123, *Harper's* CXCII (January), 36–39. Entitled in Lee as "Train Travel."

C532 "Yankee Seafarer, Companion of Capt. Cook," *NYHT Book* XXII (January 13), 3. Review of Helen Augur, *Passage to Glory*.

C533 Review of Henry Miller, *The Air Conditioned Nightmare*, *NYT Book* (January 27), 5.

*C534 The Easy Chair #124, *Harper's* CXCII (February), 123–126. Entitled in Lee as "The Civil War." Reprinted as "The War of Rebellion" in *The Easy Chair*, 151–158.

C535 "Mark Twain's 'Letter from the Recording Angel,'" *Harper's* CXCII (February), 106–109. Introduction to the story.

C536 "Mountain Time," *Collier's* CXVII (February 2), 11–13+; (February 9), 20–21+; (February 16) 30–48; (February 23) 17+; (March 2) 18+. (See A16.)

C537 "The Other Side of Some Mark Twain Stories," *NYHT Book* XXII (February 10), 3. Review of Samuel Charles Webster, editor, *Mark Twain, Business Man*.

*C538 The Easy Chair #125, *Harper's* CXCII (March), 234–237. Entitled in Lee as "The Civil War." Reprinted as "The Confederate Anachronism" in *The Easy Chair*, 159–166.

C539 "A Revaluation," *Improvement Era* 49 (March), 154. This is a reprint of "A Revaluation" printed in *Rocky Mountain Review* (Autumn 1945).

C540 "Hot Seat," *Harper's* CXCII (April) unpaged. In the "Personal & Otherwise" column.

C541 The Easy Chair #126, *Harper's* CXCII (April), 309–312. Entitled in Lee as "Mark Twain."

C542 The Easy Chair #127, *Harper's* CXCII (May), 462–465. Entitled in Lee as "George Catlin and Bill Cody."

C543 "An Englishman Accomplishes the Impossible," *NYHT Book* XXII (May 12), 3. Review of Graham Hutton, *Midwest at Noon*.

*C544 The Easy Chair #128, *Harper's* CXCII (June), 510–513. Entitled in Lee as "Anti-vivisection."

C545 "The Decision in the *Strange Fruit* Case: The Obscenity Statute in Massachusetts," *NEQ* XIX (June), 147–183.

*C546 "When the Goths Took Harvard," *NYHT Book* XXII (June 30), 2. Review of Helen Howe, *We Happy Few.*

C547 The Easy Chair #129, *Harper's* CXCIII (July), 28–31. Entitled in Lee as "Meditation on State of Nation."

C548 The Easy Chair #130, *Harper's* CXCIII (August), 126–129. Entitled in Lee as "Western Trip, Impressions and Experiences."

C549 "Fenimore Cooper's Further Literary Offenses," *NEQ* XIX (September), 291–301. DeVoto introduces the first publication of this Mark Twain manuscript.

C550 The Easy Chair #131, *Harper's* CXCIII (September), 229–232. Entitled in Lee as "Western Trip, Impressions and Experiences."

C551 The Easy Chair #132, *Harper's* CXCIII (October), 313–316. Entitled in Lee as "Western Trip, Impressions and Experiences."

C552 "A Great Explorer of the West," *NYHT Book* XXIII (October 6), 6. Review of Stanley Vestal, *Jim Bridger: Mountain Man.*

C553 "Wake Up and Meet These Great Americans," *NYHT Book* XXIII (October 27), 3. Review of Stewart H. Holbrook, *Lost Men of American History.*

C554 The Easy Chair #133, *Harper's* CXCIII (November), 430–433. Entitled in Lee as "Western Trip, Impressions and Experiences."

C555 "Westward — The Passion of Three Centuries," *NYHT Book* XXIII (November 10), 7. Review of Jeannette Mirsky, *The Westward Crossings.*

C556 "The Nebraska Heart of Boston," *NYHT Book* XXIII (November 24), 4. Review of Frances W. Dahl and Charles W. Morton, *Dahl's Boston.*

C557 "The Anxious West," *Harper's* CXCIII (December), 481–491.

C558 The Easy Chair #134, *Harper's* CXCIII (December), 537–540. Entitled in Lee as "Election Forecast: Living Costs."

C559 "The Trail That Blazed America's Way West," *NYHT Book* XXIII (December 15), 5. Review of The Editors of *Look, The Santa Fe Trail*.

C560 "The Glamour of Montana in Its Past and Present," *NYHT Book* XXIII (December 22), 2. Review of Joseph Kinsey Howard, editor, *Montana Margins*.

1947

C561 The Easy Chair #135, *Harper's* CXCIV (January), 45–48. Entitled in Lee as "The West."

C562 "The West Against Itself," *Harper's* CXCIV (January), 1–13. Reprinted in *The Easy Chair*, 231–256.

C563 The Easy Chair #136, *Harper's* CXCIV (February), 126–129. Entitled in Lee as "Movies and Psychiatry."

C564 "John Steinbeck's Bus Ride into the Hills," *NYHT Book* XXIII (February 16), 1+. Review of John Steinbeck, *The Wayward Bus*.

C565 The Easy Chair #137, *Harper's* CXCIV (March), 222–225. Entitled in Lee as "Writing and the Professors."

C566 The Easy Chair #138, *Harper's* CXCIV (April), 332–335. Entitled in Lee as "Railroad Travel." Reprinted in *Reader's Digest* (July), 119–121.

C567 "The Great American Desert of Salt Water," *NYHT Book* XXIII (April 20), 5. Review of Dale L. Morgan, *The Great Salt Lake*.

C568 The Easy Chair #139, *Harper's* CXCIV (May) 408–411. Entitled in Lee as "Literary Censorship."

C569 Review of Townsend Scudder, *Concord: American Town, America in Books* (May), first issue, no page number.

C570 Review of Clifford Dowdy, *Experiment in Rebellion, America in Books* (History Book Club) (May), first issue, no page number.

C571 "Writing for Money," *The Writer* vol. 60, no. 5 (May), 183–187.

*C572 "Marco Polo's Ford," *W Day* (May), 28–29+.

C573 "Queen City of the Plains and Peaks," *Pacific Spectator* vol. I, no. 2 (Spring), 162–174.

*C574 "Historian on Tour," *W Day* (June), 38–39+.

*C575 "The National Parks," *Fortune* XXXV (June), 120–135.

C576 The Easy Chair #140, *Harper's* CXCIV (June), 543–546. Entitled in Lee as "The Western Land Grab."

C577 "Club's First Dividend 'The Stuff of Enchantment,'" *America in Books* vol. I, no. 2 (June), no page numbers.

C578 The Easy Chair #141, *Harper's* CXCV (July), 26–29. Entitled in Lee as "Book Reviewing."

C579 "Club's Dividend for August Called 'The Stuff of Enchantment,'" *America in Books* vol. I, no. 3 (July).

*C580 "Roadside Meeting," *W Day* (July), 34–35+.

*C581 "Night Crossing," *W Day* (August), 28–29+.

C582 The Easy Chair #142, *Harper's* CXCV (August), 156–159. Entitled in Lee as "Sex Education in Colleges, 1926 and Today."

C583 "A Hank of Tall Yarns, Folklore and Fantasy," *NYHT Book* XXIV (August 24), 5. Review of Ben C. Clough, editor, *The American Imagination at Work*.

C584 "S.R.L. Founder," *SRL* XXX (August 30), 11–12. Review of Henry Seidel Canby, *American Memoir*.

C585 "Doctors along the Boardwalk," *Harper's* CXCV (September), 215–224. Reprinted in *The Easy Chair*, 85–102.

C586 The Easy Chair #143, *Harper's* CXCV (September), 247–250. Entitled in Lee as "Radio Methods Are a Mistake."

C587 "Adventurer Too Soon," *Pacific Spectator* vol. I, no. 4 (Autumn). Prepublication of Chapter X of *Across the Wide Missouri*.

C588 The Easy Chair #144, *Harper's* CXCV (October), 353–356. Entitled in Lee as "Immediate Future of American Writing."

C589 "Our Unpremeditated War with Mexico," *NYHT Book* XXIV (October 26), 7. Review of Alfred Hoyt Bill, *Rehearsal for Conflict.*

C590 Review of Clarence D. Jackson, *Picture Maker of the Old West, America in Books* (October), no page number.

C591 Review of A. R. M. Lower, *Colony to Nation, America in Books* (October), no page number.

C592 The Easy Chair #145, *Harper's* CXCV (November), 434–437. Entitled in Lee as "Bread Loaf Writer's Conference."

C593 "Those Two Immortal Boys," *W Day* (November), 38–39+.

C594 "Club Dividend for December Called 'Riotously Funny, Irresistible,' " *America in Books* vol. I, no. 7 (November), no page number.

C595 Review of Robert Kinkaid, *The Wilderness Road, America in Books* vol. I, no. 7 (November), no page number.

C596 The Easy Chair #146, *Harper's* CXCV (December), 515–518. Entitled in Lee as "Books in the Development of a Philosophy."

*C597 "Explorers Who Brought In the Northwest," *NYHT Book* XXIV (December 21), 1–2. Review of *John Bakeless, Lewis and Clark.*

C598 "Editorially Speaking," *America in Books* vol. I, no. 8 (December).

1948

*C599 The Easy Chair #147, *Harper's* CXCVI (January), 28–31. Entitled in Lee as "U.S. Forest Service and Western Land Grab."

C600 "Editorially Speaking," *America in Books* vol. I, no. 9 (January), no page number.

C601 "I Had the Funniest Dream Last Night," *W Day* (February), 46.

C602 The Easy Chair #148, *Harper's* CXCVI (February), 146–

149. Entitled in Lee as "Reply to Cyril Connolly."

C603 "Editorially Speaking," *America in Books* vol. II, no. 2 (February), 2.

C604 Review of Paul Wellman, *Death on Horseback, America in Books* vol. II, no. 2 (February), 3, 6, 8.

C605 The Easy Chair #149, *Harper's* CXCVI (March), 250–253. Entitled in Lee as "Drinking Made Whimsical." Reprinted in *The Hour* with changes, 62–70.

C606 "Talking Point," *Reader's Digest* (March), 94.

C607 "Editorially Speaking," *America in Books* vol. II, no. 3 (March), 2.

C608 "April Dividend on American Classic," *America in Books* vol. II, no. 3 (March), 6.

*C609 "More Americans Than Not," *NYHT Book* XXIV (March 28), 4. Review of Geoffrey Gorer, *The American People.*

C610 Review of Clarence P. Jackson, *Picture Maker of the Old West: William H. Jackson, American Historical Review* LIII no. 3 (April), 646–650.

C611 "Injustice," *Harper's* CXCVI (April). Letter to the editor.

C612 The Easy Chair #150, *Harper's* CXCVI (April), 313–316. Entitled in Lee as "Writing and Reading."

C613 "Editorially Speaking," *America in Books* vol. II, no. 4 (April), 2.

C614 The Easy Chair #151, *Harper's* CXCVI (May), 441–444. Entitled in Lee as "Gifford Pinchot's *Breaking New Ground.*"

C615 "Editorially Speaking," *America in Books* vol. II, no. 5 (May), 2.

C616 Review of Richard Lillard, *The Great Forest, America in Books* vol. II, no. 5 (May), 3–5.

C617 The Easy Chair #152, *Harper's* CXCVI (June), 553–556. Entitled in Lee as "Comment on the Kinsey Report."

C618 "Peter Pan, U.S.A.," *W Day* (June), 33+.

C619 The Easy Chair #153, *Harper's* CXCVII (July), 108–112.

Entitled in Lee as "Forest Service and Public Land Grants." Reprinted as "Statesmen on the Lam" in *The Easy Chair*, 283–291.

C620 "Sacred Cows and Public Lands," *Harper's* CXCVII (July), 44–55. Reprinted in *The Easy Chair*, 257–282.

C621 "The Desert Threat," *University of Colorado Bulletin* XLVIII (July), 3–4, 6–10. (See D31.)

C622 The Easy Chair #154, *Harper's* CXCVII (August), 53–57. Entitled in Lee as "Eulogy of a Historian."

C623 "Crisis of Man in Relation to His Environment," *NYHT Book* XXIV (August 8), 1–2. Review of William Vogt, *Road to Survival.*

C624 "The Good Teacher," *W Day* (September), 47+.

C625 The Easy Chair #155, *Harper's* CXCVII (September), 97–100. Entitled in Lee as "Sigmund Freud and W. H. Auden."

C626 "Conservation and the Coming Crisis," *New York Herald Tribune* (October 11).

C627 The Easy Chair #156, *Harper's* CXCVII (October), 89–92. Entitled in Lee as "Touring New England."

C628 "What Land Policy for America?" Annual Forum, *New York Herald Tribune* (October 18), reprint of speech. (See D33.)

C629 "What Counts Is the Job," *The Writer* vol. 61, no. 10 (October), 326–328. Reprinted from *Harper's* "The Easy Chair" (April).

C630 The Easy Chair #157, *Harper's* CXCVII (November), 57–60. Entitled in Lee as "Dude Ranches in the Berkshires."

C631 The Easy Chair #158, *Harper's* CXCVII (December), 98–101. Entitled in Lee as "Four-Letter Words."

C632 "Reply to a Reply," *Harper's* CXCVII (December), 17+. Letter to the editor.

*C633 "Enigmatic Friend of Indians," *NYHT Book* XXV (December 19), 6. Review of Lloyd Haberly, *Pursuit of the Horizon.*

1949

C634 "For Public Control of Public Lands," *The Land* (Winter 1948–49), 593–594.

C635 "Water Runs Downhill," *W Day* (January), 42–43+.

C636 The Easy Chair #159, *Harper's* CXCVIII (January), 94–97. Entitled in Lee as "Welsh Indians."

C637 The Easy Chair #160, *Harper's* CXCVIII (February), 70–73. Entitled in Lee as "Reviews of *Made in America* and *Guard of Honor.*

C638 The Easy Chair #161, *Harper's* CXCVIII (March), 64–67. Entitled in Lee as "National Park Service."

C639 The Easy Chair #162, *Harper's* CXCVIII (April), 52–55. Entitled in Lee as "Advice to American Historians."

C640 "The Absentee-owned Economy of the West," *NYHT Book* XXV (April 10), 5. Review of Ray B. West, editor, *Rocky Mountain Cities.*

*C641 "The U.S.A.," *The International House Quarterly* XIII (Spring), 61–69.

C642 "David Copperfield and the Beanstalk," *W Day* (May), 51+.

C643 The Easy Chair #163, *Harper's* CXCVIII (May), 54–57. Entitled in Lee as "*Time* Article on Vogt Book."

C644 The Easy Chair #164, *Harper's* CXCVIII (June), 61–64. Entitled in Lee as "Correct English and Communists in Colleges."

C645 Review of Howard H. Peckham, *The Journals and Indian Paintings of George Winter, 1837–1839, Mississippi Valley Historical Review,* XXXVI (June), 136–138.

C646 The Easy Chair #165, *Harper's* CXCIX (July), 62–65. Entitled in Lee as "Literary Censorship."

C647 "The Life and Wife of a Writer," *W Day* (August), 36+. Reprinted in *Women and Children First,* by Cady Hewes, 139–151.

C648 The Easy Chair #166, *Harper's* CXCIX (August), 43–46. Entitled in Lee as "On Rereading Novels."

*C649 "Time without a Theme," *SRL* XXXII (August 6), 27–29.

C650 The Easy Chair #167, *Harper's* CXCIX (September), 76–79. Entitled in Lee as "Colleges and Un-American Activities Committee."

C651 "The Colleges, the Government and Freedom," *American Association of University Professors Bulletin* XXXV, no. 3 (Autumn), 468–475. Reprinted from The Easy Chair #167 (September).

C652 "Due Notice to the F.B.I.," The Easy Chair #168, *Harper's* CXCIX (October), 65–68. Reprinted in *The Easy Chair*, 169–176.

C653 "Restoration in the Wasatch," *The American Scholar* XVIII, No. 4 (October), 425–432.

C654 "Water Runs Downhill," *Outdoor America* vol. 14, no. 8 (October), 5–7, 10.

C655 "Derbies Are Male," by Cady Hewes, *W Day* (November). Reprinted in *Women and Children First* by Cady Hewes, 98–109.

C656 "The Spectral Evidence," The Easy Chair #169, *Harper's* CXCIX (November), 46–49.

C657 "To 1864, When Lincoln Made U. S. Grant General-in-Chief," *NYHT Book* XXVI (November 6), 3. Review of Kenneth P. Williams, *Lincoln Finds a General.*

C658 "Our Contemporary, Jonathan Edwards," *NYHT Book* XXVI (November 20), 4. Review of Perry Miller, *Jonathan Edwards.*

C659 "Due Notice —," *Harper's* CXCIX (December), 16. Letter to the editor.

C660 "For the Wayward and Beguiled," The Easy Chair #170, *Harper's* CXCIX (December), 68–71. Reprinted in *The Hour*, 27–43. Other reprints are entitled "An Appreciation of the Martini Cocktail" or "A Bit of Rhetoric on the Topic of Gin and Vermouth." (See A18.)

C661 "The Novel Is Always a Story," *The Writer* vol. 62, no. 12 (December), 395–397.

C662 "Lesson of Davis County," *Reader's Digest* (December), 89–92. Reprinted from *American Scholar*, Autumn, 1949.

1950

C663 "Parable of the Lost Chance," The Easy Chair #171, *Harper's* CC (January), 42–45. Reprinted in *The Easy Chair*, 57–64.

C664 "The Invisible Novelist," *Pacific Spectator* IV, no. 1, 30–45 (Winter), Chapter IX of *The World of Fiction*.

C665 "Professor or Professional?" *W Day* (February), 49+.

C666 "Year-end Megrims," The Easy Chair #172, *Harper's* CC (February), 27–30.

C667 "Almost Toujours Gai," The Easy Chair #173, *Harper's* CC (March), 49–52. Reprinted in *The Easy Chair*, 65–73.

C668 "The Christopherson Papers," The Easy Chair #174, *Harper's* CC (April), 97–100.

C669 "The World Wives Live In," by Cady Hewes, *W Day* (April), 35+. Reprinted in *Women and Children First* by Cady Hewes, 3–15.

C670 "A Major New Landmark in the Critical Study of the American West," *NYHT Book* XXVI (April 9), 4. Review of Henry Nash Smith, *Virgin Land*.

C671 "The Camel on the Moon," *W Day* (May), 40–41+.

C672 "Wanted, an Umpire," The Easy Chair #175, *Harper's* CC (May), 60–63.

C673 "State of the Nation (Spring)," The Easy Chair #176, *Harper's* CC (June), 78–81.

C674 "From New England the Yankee Went His Curious Way," *NYHT Book* XXVI (June 11), 1+. Review of Stewart H. Holbrook, *The Yankee Exodus*.

*C675 "Research by Air," The Easy Chair #177, *Harper's* CCI (July), 22–55. Original titles "South Pass by Air" or "Ox Team West by Air."

*C676 "We Grew Up with Danger," *W Day* (July), 27. Original title: "This Nettle, Danger."

C677 "Shall We Let Them Ruin Our National Parks?" *Post* CCXXIII (July 22), 17–19+. Reprinted in *Reader's Digest* (November), 18–24.

C678 "A Fine New Talent on Ol' Man River," *NYHT Book* XXVI (July 23), 7. Review of Richard Bissell, *A Stretch on the River*.

C679 "Our Hundred Year Plan," The Easy Chair #178, *Harper's* CCI (August), 60–64.

C680 "Ninety-day Venus," The Easy Chair #179, *Harper's* CCI (September), 93–96. Reprinted in *The Easy Chair*, 41–48.

C681 "Tame Indian, Lone Sailor," *NYT Book* (September 24), 9+. Review of Walter Van Tilburg Clark, *Watchful Gods and Other Stories*.

*C682 "The Century," *Harper's* CCI (October), 49–58. Reprinted in *The Easy Chair*, 13–30.

*C683 "The Constant Function," The Easy Chair #180, *Harper's* CCI (October), 215–220.

*C684 "Gone Are the Days," *W Day* (October), 46–47+. Original title: "The Old Home We Never Wanted."

C685 "But Sometimes They Vote Right Too," The Easy Chair #181, *Harper's* CCI (November), 64–67. Reprinted in *The Easy Chair*, 191–198.

C686 "Here Is the Civil War — America As It Really Was — Magnificent and Vile," *NYHT Book* XXVII (November 19), 5. Review of Henry Steele Commager, editor, *The Blue and the Gray*.

*C687 "The Lush Life of the Primitive Continent," *NYHT Book* XXVII (November 26), 6. Review of John Bakeless, *The Eyes of Discovery*.

C688 "Shop Talk," The Easy Chair #182, *Harper's* CCI (December), 54–57. Reprinted in *The Easy Chair*, 49–56.

C689 "On the Writing of History," *Chicago History Quarterly* II, No. 10 (Winter), 314–315. Letter to the editor.

1951

C690 "Homily for a Troubled Time," *W Day* (January), 36–37+.

C691 "Letter to a Family Doctor," The Easy Chair #183, *Harper's* CCII (January), 56–60.

*C692 "The Ex-Communists," *Atlantic* CLXXXVII (February), 61–65. Reprinted in *The Easy Chair*, 177–189.

*C693 "Men, Women and Eight Cylinders," by Cady Hewes, *W Day* (February), 39+. Reprinted in *Women and Children First* by Cady Hewes, 88–97.

C694 "Our First Testing," The Easy Chair #184, *Harper's* CCII (February), 55–58.

C695 "Two-gun Desmond Is Back," The Easy Chair #185, *Harper's* CCII (March), 48–51. Reprinted in *The Easy Chair*, 293–300.

C696 "Whiskey Is for Patriots," The Easy Chair #186, *Harper's* CCII (April), 68–71. Reprinted, with changes, in *The Hour*, 1–25.

*C697 "Why Professors Are Suspicious of Business," *Fortune* XLIII (April), 114–115+.

C698 "Documented Novel of the Old Northwest Fur Trade," *NYHT Book* XXVII (April 1), 3. Review of Walter O'Meara, *The Grand Portage*.

C699 "Spring Clearance," The Easy Chair #187, *Harper's* CCII (May), 50–53.

C700 "Dull Novels Make Dull Reading," The Easy Chair #188, *Harper's* CCII (June), 67–70.

*C701 "The Watchers on the Wall," *W Day* (June), 36+.

C702 "Your Land and Mine —," *Harper's* CCII (June), 22. Letter to the editor.

*C703 "Pocket Guide to Horse Opera," by Cady Hewes, *W Day* (July), 17+.

C704 "Foul Birds Come Abroad [sic]," The Easy Chair #189, *Harper's* CCIII (July), 48–52.

C705 "The Only Man To Paint the Rocky Mountain Fur

Trade," *NYHT Book* XXVII (July 22), 1. Review of Marvin G. Ross, *The West of Alfred Jacob Miller.*

*C706 "Listen Sister," by Fairley Blake, *Atlantic* CLXXXVIII (July), 90–92. Reprinted, with changes, in *The Hour*, 53–57, entitled "Ce qu'il faut connaître des coktels pour les hôstesses [sic]." (See A18.)

C707 "An It in the Corner," The Easy Chair #190, *Harper's* CCIII (August), 59–62. Reprinted in *The Easy Chair*, 75–82.

C708 "Ordeal by Poetry," The Easy Chair #191, *Harper's* CCIII (September), 43–46.

*C709 "Anyone Can Talk to a Genius," by Cady Hewes, *W Day* (October), 66+. Reprinted in *Women and Children First*, 110–118.

C710 "Two Points of a Joke," The Easy Chair #192, *Harper's* CCIII (October), 73–76.

C711 "A New Approach to Our History, Visual and Revealing," *NYHT Book* XXVIII (October 21), 1. Review of Marshall B. Davidson, *Life in America.*

C712 "Crusade Resumed," The Easy Chair #193, *Harper's* CCIII (November), 95–98.

*C713 "The Smoke Jumpers," *Harper's* CCIII (November), 54–61. Reprinted in *The Easy Chair*, 103–148.

C714 "Wayfarer's Daybook," The Easy Chair #194, *Harper's* CCIII (December), 44–47.

1952

C715 "The Monster in the Home," by Cady Hewes, *W Day* (January), 27+. Reprinted in *Women and Children First* by Cady Hewes, 27–38.

C716 "The Sixty-Cent Royalty," The Easy Chair #195, *Harper's* CCIV (January), 41–44.

C717 "These Lands Are Yours," *W Day* (February), 61–68+.

C718 "Why Read Dull Novels?" The Easy Chair #196, *Harper's* CCIV (February), 65–69.

C719 "The Third Floor," The Easy Chair #197, *Harper's* CCIV

(March), 43–46. Reprinted in *The Easy Chair*, 31–38.

C720 "Stevenson and the Independent Voter," The Easy Chair #198, *Harper's* CCIV (April), 62–66.

C721 "The Seventh Pocketbook," *Mademoiselle* (March), 95, 148–151.

*C722 "Personal and Otherwise," *Harper's* CCIV (April), 14. Letter to the editor.

C723 "Hurried Crossing," *W Day* (May), 64–65+.

C724 "Les Amis des Deux Fishboulettes," The Easy Chair #199, *Harper's* CCIV (May), 50–53.

C725 "Next to Reading Matter," The Easy Chair #200, *Harper's* CCIV (June), 61–64.

*C726 "Women in the Military Services," *W Day* (June), 59+.

*C727 "Transcontinental Flight," The Easy Chair #201, *Harper's* CCV (July), 47–50.

C728 "Vermont Is the Vermonters," *Reader's Digest* (July), 109–110. Reprinted from *Harper's* (n.d.).

*C729 "Flood in the Desert," The Easy Chair #202, *Harper's* CCV (August), 58–61.

C730 "Boyhood Years That Shaped Mark Twain's Great Art," *NYHT Book* XXIX (August 31), 1+. Review of Dixon Wecter, *Sam Clemens of Hannibal*.

C731 "The End of the Stalwarts," The Easy Chair #203, *Harper's* CCV (September), 78–81.

C732 "Turning Point for Lewis and Clark," *Harper's* CCV (September), 36–43. Excerpt from Chapter XI of *The Course of Empire*.

C733 "An Old Steal Refurbished," The Easy Chair #204, *Harper's* CCV (October), 65–68.

C734 "What Wendell Willkie Meant to His Party, His Country and the World," *NYHT Book* XXIX (October 12), 5. Review of Joseph Barnes, *Willkie*.

C735 "Remainder Shelf," The Easy Chair #205, *Harper's* CCV (November), 65–68.

C736 "Transcontinental Flight," *Reader's Digest* (November), 86–88.

*C737 "Masterly Report on Civil War Generalship," *NYHT*

Book XXIX (November 2), 4. Review of Kenneth P. Williams, *Lincoln Finds a General.*

*C738 "The High Country," *W Day* (December), 60–61+.

C739 "Samuel Hall, Gent," The Easy Chair #206, *Harper's* CCV (December), 53–56.

C740 "Twenty-nine Who Pictured the Old West," *NYHT Book* XXIX (December 14), 5. Review of Harold McCracken, *Portrait of the Old West.*

1953

C741 "Preliminary Forecast," The Easy Chair #207, *Harper's* CCVI (January), 52–55.

C742 "Virus Infection," by Cady Hewes, *W Day* (January), 44+. Reprinted in *Women and Children First* by Cady Hewes, 16–26.

C743 "Billion Dollar Jackpot," The Easy Chair #208, *Harper's* CCVI (February), 53–56. Reprinted in *The Easy Chair*, 301–309.

C744 "Extracts from the Speeches of the National Book Award Winners," by Archibald MacLeish, Ralph Ellison, and Bernard DeVoto, *NYHT Book* XXIX (February 15), 6.

C745 "Twenty-Hour Vigil," The Easy Chair #209, *Harper's* CCVI (March), 50–53. Reprinted in *The Easy Chair*, 135–142.

*C746 "Celebrating 150 Years of the Louisiana Purchase," *Collier's* CXXXI (March 21), 44–50+. Reprinted as *The Louisiana Purchase*, Crowell-Collier. Original title: "Traveling the Louisiana Purchase."

C747 "The Case of the Censorious Congressman," The Easy Chair #210, *Harper's* CCVI (April), 42–45. Reprinted in *The Easy Chair*, 199–206.

*C748 "The Indian All Round Us," *Reader's Digest* LXII (April), 61–64.

C749 "The New England Hill Country," *W Day* (April), 58–59+.

C750 "The Sturdy Corporate Homesteader," The Easy Chair

#211, *Harper's* CCVI (May), 57–60. Reprinted in *The Easy Chair*, 311–319.

*C751 "Topic One," by Cady Hewes, *W Day* (May), 45+. Reprinted in *Women and Children First* by Cady Hewes, 39–52.

*C752 "Ore for the Rouge," *Lincoln and Mercury Times* V, no. 3 (May–June), 21–24.

C753 "The Visual Instrument," The Easy Chair #212, *Harper's* CCVI (June), 49–52.

C754 "TV, a Minority Report," *Reader's Digest* (June), 78–80.

C755 "Heading for the Last Roundup," The Easy Chair #213, *Harper's* CCVII (July), 49–52. Reprinted in *The Easy Chair*, 321–328.

*C756 "Homicide in the Home," *W Day* (July), 48+. Reprinted in *Women and Children First* by Cady Hewes, 321–328.

C757 Review of A. P. Nasatir, editor, *Before Lewis and Clark: Documents Illustrating the History of the Missouri, 1785–1804,* American Historical Review LVIII, no. 4 (July), 933–935.

*C758 "Mr. Ford's Favorite Town — Dearborn, Michigan," *Ford Times* vol. 45, no. 7 (July), 16–21.

C759 "Summer Preface," The Easy Chair #214, *Harper's* CCVII (August), 54–57. Pages 54–55 reprinted as "Comment on a Technique" in *The Easy Chair*, 207–210.

C760 "Motel Town," The Easy Chair #215, *Harper's* CCVII (September), 45–48. Reprinted in *The Easy Chair*, 119–126.

C761 "Playtime Paradise," *W Day* (September), 63+.

C762 "Let's Close the National Parks," The Easy Chair #216, *Harper's* CCVII (October), 49–52.

C763 "Notes on Western Travel," The Easy Chair #217, *Harper's* CCVII (November), 45–48.

C764 "Always Be Drastically Independent," The Easy Chair #218, *Harper's* CCVII (December), 42–45.

C765 "Our Great West, Boom or Bust?" *Collier's* CXXXII (December 25), 46–50+.

C766 "Traveling the Louisiana Purchase," *Ford Times* Vol. 45, No. 12 (December), 2–8. (The March, 1954, issue of *Ford Times* contained a letter written by DeVoto to the editor in answer to questions raised by readers of this article.)

1954

C767 "My Career As a Lawbreaker," The Easy Chair #219, *Harper's* CCVIII (January), 8+.

*C768 "That Southern Inferiority Complex," *Post* CCXXXVI (January 16), 27+. Original title: "Who Has Slighted the South?"

*C769 "Disaster Long Ago," *W Day* (February), 44–45+.

C770 "Parks and Pictures," The Easy Chair #220, *Harper's* CCVIII (February), 12+.

*C771 "What Makes a Real Martini?" *True Magazine* XXXIV (February), 54+. Original title: "The Martini Unadorned."

*C772 "The Impatient Patient," by Cady Hewes, *W Day* (March). Reprinted in *Women and Children First* by Cady Hewes, 53–56.

C773 "Intramural Giveaway," The Easy Chair #221, *Harper's* CCVIII (March), 10–11+.

*C774 "My Wife Is Many Cooks," by Cady Hewes, *W Day* (April), 80+. Reprinted in *Women and Children First* by Cady Hewes, 211–220. Original title: "An Artist in the Kitchen."

C775 "Norwalk and Points West," The Easy Chair #222, *Harper's* CCVIII (April), 10–15. Reprinted in *The Easy Chair*, 211–220.

C776 "DeVoto's New England," *Harper's* CCVIII (May), 61–67.

C777 "Fantasy at Noonday," The Easy Chair #223, *Harper's* CCVIII (May), 8–13.

C778 "Follow Any Road," *W Day* (May), 36–37+.

*C779 "Victory at Sea," The Easy Chair #224, *Harper's* CCVIII (June), 8–11+. Reprinted in *The Easy Chair*, 143–150.

*C780 "The Grand Coulee Is Grand," *NYHT Book* XXX (June 27), 12. Review of George Sundborg, *Hail Columbia*.

C781 "Alias Nero Wolfe," The Easy Chair #225, *Harper's* CCIX (July), 8–9+.

C782 "Cambridge Man," *Holiday* XVI (July), 33. Autobiographical letter.

*C783 "The Link," by Frank Gilbert, *Esquire* (July). Original title: "The Hidden." Short story.

*C784 "Wild West," *Holiday* XVI (July), 34–43+. Reprinted in *Reader's Digest* (September), 115–120. Original title: "Western Paradox."

C785 "Conservation: Down and on the Way Out," *Harper's* CCIX (August), 66–74. Reprinted in *The Easy Chair*, 329–347.

*C786 "Yankee Reserve," The Easy Chair #226, *Harper's* CCIX (August), 8–9+.

C787 "And Fractions Drive Me Mad," The Easy Chair #227, *Harper's* CCIX (September), 10–11+.

C788 "New England Revisited," *The Lamp* XXXVI (September), 20–23.

C789 "Culture at Two Bits," The Easy Chair #228, *Harper's* CCIX (October), 8–10+.

*C790 "The White-Water Riverman," *Holiday* XVI (October), 23–24+.

C791 "In the Horse Latitudes," The Easy Chair #229, *Harper's* CCIX (November), 8–9+.

C792 "Phaëthon on Gunsmoke Trail," The Easy Chair #230, *Harper's* CCIX (December), 10–11+.

C793 "Yankee Grand Tour," *Ford Times, New England Journeys* #2, 9–12.

1955

C794 "One-Way Partnership Derailed," The Easy Chair #231, *Harper's* CCX (January), 12–15+.

C795 "Service in Four-color Gravure," The Easy Chair #232, *Harper's* CCX (February), 10–12+.

C796 "Airlines Need a Lesson in Traveler Relations," *Time* (February 14), 23. Reprinted from *Harper's* (n.d.).

C797 "Hazards of the Road," The Easy Chair #233, *Harper's* CCX (March), 14–19.

C798 "Guilt by Distinction," The Easy Chair #234, *Harper's* CCX (April), 14–15+. Reprinted in *The Easy Chair*, 221–228.

C799 "Current Comic Strips," The Easy Chair #235, *Harper's* CCX (May), 8–9+.

C800 "The Zippered Egg Boiler," by Cady Hewes, *W Day* (May), 29+. Reprinted in *Women and Children First* by Cady Hewes, 76–87.

C801 "The Reference Shelf," *Writer* LXVIII (June), 185–188.

C802 "For the Record," The Easy Chair #236, *Harper's* CCX (June), 12–13+.

*C803 Review of Samuel Eliot Morison, editor, *The Parkman Reader*, *NEQ* XXVIII (June), 263–267.

*C804 "New England," *Holiday* XVII (July), 34–47. Original title: "The Yankee Republic."

C805 "Peter and Wendy in the Revolution," The Easy Chair #237, *Harper's* CCXI (July), 10–12+.

C806 "On the Record," *Harper's* CCXI (August), 4. Letter to the editor.

*C807 "Spread of an Infection," The Easy Chair #238, *Harper's* CCXI (August), 12–13+.

C808 "An Inference Regarding the Expedition of Lewis and Clark." Reprinted from the *Proceedings* of the American Philosophical Society, vol. 99 (August 30), 185–194.

C809 "And the DAR," *Harper's* CCXI (September), 6.

*C810 "Hell's Half Acre, Mass." The Easy Chair #239, *Harper's* CCXI (September), 10–11+.

C811 "Outdoor Metropolis," The Easy Chair #240, *Harper's* CCXI (October), 12–13+.

*C812 "Number 241," The Easy Chair #241, *Harper's* CCXI (November), 10–17. Reprinted in *The Easy Chair*, 3–11.

*C813 "Birth of an Art," The Easy Chair #242, *Harper's* CCXI (December), 8–9+.

C814 "Essence of New England–Lincoln Gap, Vermont," *New England Journeys* #3, 10–12.

C815 "Tour Boston on Foot," *Ford Times, New England Journeys* #3, 56–57.

1956

*C816 "Beating the Bali Hai Racket," The Easy Chair #243, *Harper's* CCXI (January), 10–12+.

.*C817 "Heavy, Heavy, What Hangs Over?" *Holiday* XIX (March), 37–38+. Original title: "Boredom de Luxe."

*C818 "Good Place To Grow In," *Lincoln-Mercury Times* VIII (March–April), 1–3. Original title: "Ogden." (See B1.)

*C819 "Two Days in Washington," *W Day* (March), 58–62.

*C820 "Bread Loaf, Vermont," *Ford Times* XLVIII (May), 2–6. Reprinted in *New England Journeys* #4.

*C821 "Uncle Sam's Campgrounds," *Ford Times* XLVIII (June), 2–10.

*C822 "Let me tell you about the Wasatch," *Lincoln-Mercury Times* VII (July–August), 12–15. Original title: "The Wasatch."

*C823 "Your National Forests," *Holiday* XX (August), 93+.

*C824 "Roads of the Past," *The Lamp* XXXVIII (Fall), 10–15. Original title: "Early Highways of the East."

*C825 "Coolidge's Grave in Plymouth," *New England Journeys* #4. Original title: "Plymouth Cemetery."

1957

C826 "DeVoto's Letters from Harvard," by Carolyn Hoggan, the *Pen* (Spring), 19–21.

1958

C827 "Astor and Astoria," *American Heritage* IX (August), 61. Excerpt from *Course of Empire*, 8–58.

1959

*C828 "The Champlain Corridor," *Ford Times* LI (February), 10–13.

D. Lectures — Speeches — Broadcasts

DeVoto lectured frequently and appeared often on radio and television. He wrote Clifton Fadiman in March, 1945, ". . . there is practically no organization in Greater New England left that has not listened to me." The editors have not tried to compile a complete list of his multitudinous engagements. This very fragmentary list was obtained from statements in his correspondence and from announcements and brochures contained in his papers. It is included here as indication of the variety of places in which he spoke and subjects which concerned him. Title, place, medium, and exact date are given where they are known.

The asterisk (*) denotes a manuscript or typescript copy in the DeVoto Papers.

1935

D1 "Mark Twain's America." Books of the Day, Lecture VI, Salt Lake City, Utah.

*D2 "Mark Twain: The Ink of History." Address delivered at Columbia, Missouri (December 6). Printed in *Forays and Rebuttals*, 348–372.

1936

*D3 "Mark Twain and the Limits of Criticism." Paper read before the American Literature section of the Modern Language Association (January 1). Printed in *Forays and Rebuttals*, 373–403.

1937

D4 Address at Middlebury College, Vermont (April). Printed in the *Middlebury College News Letter*. (See C371.)
*D5 New York Times Book Fair.
D6 Harvard Committee on Extra-curricular Study of American History. Three radio broadcasts (December).
*   1) A Problem: The Civil War.
*   2) Attitudes of Fiction.
*   3) The Materials of History.

1939

D7 "World of Tomorrow." Writers Program.

1940

*D8 "New Light on Mark Twain." William Vaughan Moody Lectures: University of Chicago (March 5). Printed with changes in *Mark Twain at Work* as "The Symbols of Despair." (See A10.) (In the introduction to *Mark Twain in Eruption*, page xx, DeVoto refers to an article written for *Harper's* and personally published in the January, 1940, issue, an article which was enlarged for the Moody lecture. Such an article does not appear in the January, 1940, *Harper's*. In *Mark Twain at Work*, page 143, DeVoto states that "The Symbols of Despair" was printed "here" for the first time.)

1941

D9 Eight lectures at the Lowell Institute. (See A12.)
1) "Year of Decision: Great American Desert and Some People."
2) "Build Thee More Stately Mansions: Expansionism, the Industrial Revolution and War with Mexico."
3) "Let My People Go: The Mormon Migration."
4) "Oh Susanna: The American as Emigrant."
5) "John Doe on the Oregon Trail: Further Narratives of Emigration."
6) "Military Conquest: The Doniphan Expedition and the Bear Flag Operetta."
7) "Trail's End: The Donner Party and Other Endings."
8) "American Empire: What the Year of Decision Decided."
D10 "The Waste Land and the Irresponsibles." Harvard Phi Beta Kappa address. (June 20.)

1942

D11 Three speeches on the war.
*   1) Untitled.
*   2) "From the Apprenticeship of 1917."
*   3) "The Home Town Front."
D12 Commencement address: Goddard College.
D13 "Responsible Citizenship Makes Responsible Government." Address to the Biennial Convention of the National League of Women Voters (April 28).

1943

D14 Speech at Polish Institute of Arts and Sciences in America.
D15 Five Patten Foundation lectures: University of Indiana. (See A13.)
1) "Oh, Lost America." (March 3.)
2) "The Interpreter's House." (March 10.)

3) "Waste Land." (March 17.)
4) "But Is It Art?" (March 29.)
5) "The Meal in the Firkin." (March 31.)

1944

D16 University Club speech. (February 3.)
D17 Whitman broadcast. (February 11.)
D18 "Tom Sawyer," *Invitation to Learning*. Radio. (June 4.)
*D19 Democratic campaign speech.
D20 Speech at Williams College. (November.)
D21 Speech at Charles Street Forum. (December 10.)
*D22 Intermission speeches: radio broadcasts of the New York Philharmonic. (December 17, December 31.)

1945

D23 Two untitled lectures on World War II.
   1) Veterans.
   2) German defeat.
D24 Bookbuilders of Boston. Speech. (February 20.)
D25 Lecture at Cambridge. (March 4.)
*D26 "Sense or Censorship," *Ford Hall Forum, Boston*. (April 1.)
D27 *Information Please*. Radio. (June 3.)
D28 "Autobiography of Lincoln Steffens," *Invitation to Learning*. Radio. (August 5.)

1947

D29 Vermilion, South Dakota. Lecture. (November.)

1948

D30 Columbia University. Lecture. (January 6.)
*D31 "The Desert Threat." Commencement address, University of Colorado. (See C621.)

*D32 Speech for the Denver Conservation Conference. (September.)

*D33 "What Land Policy for America?" Television. New York Herald Tribune Forum. (October 18.) (See C628.)

1949

*D34 "U.S.A." *Living America Series.* (January 9.)

*D35 "Literature and the American Historian." Pembroke College. Speech.

*D36 "Of Men and Books." Boston. (September 1.)

1950

D37 "The Welsh Indians." Lecture at Cooper Union. (December.)

1951

D38 Lectured in Montana for ten days.

1952

*D39 Campaign Speeches of Adlai Stevenson used at St. Louis, Fort Dodge, Seattle, Cheyenne, Detroit, Albuquerque, and other unidentified locations.

1953

*D40 Speech on Conservation and Grazing.

1954

D41 "The Give Aways." New Mexico. Speech.

*D42 Campaign speech. Seattle.

*D43 Commencement address. Goddard College.

D44 "Some American Symbols." The City Club of Cleveland. (November 13.)

D45 "From an Editor's Chair." The Lyceum-Tulane Association. (November 18.)

1955

D46 "An Inference Regarding the Expedition of Lewis and Clark." Penrose Memorial Lecture to the American Philosophical Society. Printed in the *Proceedings* of the American Philosophical Society. (See C808.)

*D47 "Mesa Verde," *Adventure Series*. Television. (November 13.)

D48 Three television films.

*   1) "The People's Heritage."

*   2) "Mountains on the Move."

*   3) "Stories in the Rocks."

Undated

*D49 "Mountain Time," The Veteran's Theatre of the Air. Radio. (The DeVoto Papers include the radio script and photographs of the actors.)

E. Unpublished or Unidentified Manuscripts

THE DEVOTO PAPERS contain the following manuscripts and typescripts which are either unpublished or unidentified. It has been difficult to distinguish the published from the unpublished work of DeVoto in manuscript form for he rarely dated a finished piece and he did not indicate the name of the periodical which published the article. The printed article often carries a different title from the one designated on the manuscript by DeVoto. Dates and titles are given where they are known.

Poetry — Unpublished

(Undated but probably written while a student.
Titles and/or first lines are listed.)

E1 "Heading West Again." "I am heading for the hills and I'm happy to be going,"

E2 "Septenaries." "The eastern sky was flushing red behind the huddled peaks"

E3 "Concerning a Young Woman." "The Lady I am singing of"

E4 "Chief Three Bears." "Why is the sunlight cold when it falls on the south-open door of my tepee?" (A notation at the end "by Elliott C. Lincoln.")

E5 "Grief of Love Stood by My Chair."

E6 "Midsummer Repertory." "Comes curtain-fall upon our summer's play"

E7 "Now you, who rode with me beneath the peaks"

E8 "Twilight has fallen, a curtain let down from the arch of the mountains,"

E9 "Forspent with sin I bow, O Nazarene,"

E10 "Mea Lesbia, gaudeamus —." "Was it six years ago? I know that summer"

E11 "The quiet afternoon will be your friend,"

E12 "Florian Sings." A sequence of six poems.
"You heard me sing, M'sieur, me, Florian?"
"Song." "Life is a willow-leaf"
"Serenade." "Florian sends you a rose to wear"
"Nocturne." "The wind is hushed, the leaves are still"
"Cavatina." "So wistfully she said good-bye"
"Sonnet." "If I have fallen asleep and dreamed too long"

E13 "From 'The River and the Idol,' A Sonnet Sequence."
    I "I do not ask you, dear, for anything;"
    II "Come out with me into the April weather;"
    V "Could I bear sorrow with me to the height"
    VII "Midsummer beckons us beside the river,"
    X "If there were God, He who had made the day,"

XI "Dear, you are strong and I am very weak,"
XII "Beloved, may I tell you? In the night,"

Play

E14 "The Mormons."

Short Stories

E15 "Martin Would A-fishing Go," September, 1919.
E16 "A Stranger Comes to the Well," October 14, 1919.
E17 "The Burning Bush," October 28, 1919. (See A2.)
E18 "Misericordia" (one page sketch), November 1, 1919.
E19 Story involving George Washington, no title, December 16, 1919.
E20 "Part Three Gordon Abbey, 1910–1922." (Part of an early version of either *The House of Sun-Goes-Down* or *The Crooked Mile*. See also E90.)
E21 "Premature Midnight," purchased by *Cosmopolitan*.
E22 "The Baron's Right," by John August.
E23 "J. Harrod."
E24 "Over the Mountain," by John August.
E25 "Suspicion of Violence," by John August.

Articles and Essays

E26 Preface, December 28, 1919.
E27 "Resurreximus," September 29, 1919.
E28 "Up from the Oyster?" October, 1919.
E29 "Sunbeams from Cucumbers," October 11, 1919.
E30 "There Was a Man," October 18, 1919.
E31 "Between Quintana and the Deep Blue Sea."
E32 "Suggestions to Mr. Lincoln," November 1, 1919.
E33 "Chautauqua and the Desert Stars."
E34 "Arise, Be of Good Cheer," November 1, 1919.
E35 " 'La-Plata Mines To Be Re-opened' — The Home Town Newspaper," October 25, 1919.

E36 "A Bas Les Rollo's."

E37 "Defect of Me. Slingerland's Quality," November 15, 1919.

E38 "A Beggar at the Gate," November 22, 1919.

E39 "An Undergraduate on Education."

E40 "A Humanist's Dilemma."

E41 "While the Philistines Jostle."

E42 "A Most Useful Engine for the Catching of Owls, or, The Usual Manner of Witches," December 2, 1919.

E43 "Bowing and Dodging Turnips."

E44 "— of the Season," December 15, 1919.

E45 One page article on the "New Era."

E46 "The Literature on the American Experiment," April, 1920.

E47 "Henry Adams' Dynamic Theory of History," May, 1920. Awarded the Wister Prize — Harvard, 1920.

E48 "Interlude, The Death of a Pioneer."

E49 "Sex and the Co-ed," by John August. Purchased by *The American Mercury*, and intended to have been used as the lead article in the May, 1926, issue. However, the "Hat-rack" article had appeared in the April issue and had been denounced as "immoral" by the New England Watch and Ward Society. Fearful of losing the second class mail privilege if another "immoral" article appeared, Mencken withdrew the DeVoto article.

E50 "Far Western Trails," purchased by *The Lamp*.

E51 "Fair Weather Children," purchased by *Woman's Day*.

E52 "Women and Their Roles," purchased by *Woman's Day*.

E53 "The Protocol of Touring," purchased by *The Lamp*.

E54 "James P. Beckwourth," 1927.

E55 "History Books of 1947."

E56 "Fire Fighting by the Book," also titled "Jack of 465 Trades."

E57 "Horse Opera in Modern Dress."

E58 "Kiwanis Saves a Watershed," written for *Look*.

E59 "The Range War, 1951."

E60 "Westward the Course of Empire."

E61 "After Adjudication, Agitation."

E62 "Frontier Family Medicine."

E63 "Esso Touring Aids Program."

E64 "The Intermountain West."

E65 "The Future of the West."

E66 "Remember about the West."

E67 "Melville."

E68 "The Historical Novel."

E69 "The Present Status of American Fiction."

E70 "A Note on Hamlet," written for *This Week*.

E71 "I Can't Quite Hear You, Dr." An answer to an article by Joseph A. Brandt, *Harper's*, March, 1946.

E72 "The SAC Beneath the Fangs." Proposed "Easy Chair" on Senator Joseph A. McCarthy.

E73 "Flats Fixed at Mert's Bar-B-Q."

E74 "The Railroads Lose $400," written for "The Easy Chair," 1937.

E75 "Fiction Is Vicious."

E76 "What to Tell the Child."

E77 Biographical sketch of A. B. Guthrie.

E78 A salute to the Lewiston (Idaho) *Morning Tribune*.

Reviews

E79 *The Watchful Gods and Other Stories* by Walter Van Tilburg Clark, 1942. (Reviewed from galleys.)

E80 *A Mormon Frontier* (Desert Saints. The Mormon Frontier in Utah) by Nels Anderson.

E81 *Grant and His Captains* by C. E. Macartney.

E82 *The People, Yes* by Carl Sandburg.

E83 *The Naked and the Dead* by Norman Mailer.

E84 *Mark Twain Dictionary* by Caroline Thomas Harnsberger.

E85 *The Mystery of a "Public Man"* by Frank Maloy Anderson.

E86 *The Big Sky* by A. B. Guthrie.

Undated Fragments

E87 Notes for novels.

E88 Article on leaving Camp Lee after World War I. Ca.1919.

E89 Essays notebook in manuscript:
 "What Kind of Revolution?"
 "Thinking about America."
 Story fragment.
 Untitled essay on Ogden. (See B1.)

E90 Pages from first chapter of a novel, "In the Valley." November 11, 1919. (Part of an early version of either *The House of Sun-Goes-Down* or *The Crooked Mile*. See also E20.)

E91 "Conservation and S1149." Eight pages, addressed to a government committee.

E92 Proposal for two articles on forest fires.

E93 Proposal for article on White Mountain National Forest.

E94 "The Trail of Lewis and Clark." Two versions, 18 pages.

E95 Notes for work on the *"Strange Fruit* Case."

E96 "The River and the Idol." Essays, notebook on manuscript. (See also E13.)
 a) "What a Wise Man Says."
 b) "A Canal under the Sun."
 c) "The Girl without a Palate."
 d) "Uranian Venus."
 e) "Poplars for Honor."

E97 Three story fragments, no titles.

E98 Seven short stories, no titles. (Three in manuscript.)

E99 Article on "Fishing."

E100 Two drafts of an article intended for "The Easy Chair."

E101 Article on "Scholars."

E102 "Matthiessen and the Progressive Party." An unfinished letter to the *New York Herald Tribune* dated April 4, 1950.